MY SCREWS
ARE LOOSE

MY SCREWS ARE LOOSE

A Story of Triumph Over Tragedy

Nichole Thomas

MY SCREWS ARE LOOSE
A STORY OF TRIUMPH OVER TRAGEDY

iUniverse books may be ordered through booksellers or by contacting:

iUniverse
1663 Liberty Drive
Bloomington, IN 47403
www.iuniverse.com
1-800-Authors (1-800-288-4677)

Photographer: Frank Carnaggio Photography
Cover design and graphics: Joseph Camp Studios

ISBN: 978-1-5320-8425-6 (sc)
ISBN: 978-1-5320-8424-9 (hc)
ISBN: 978-1-5320-8426-3 (e)

Library of Congress Control Number: 2019914833

Print information available on the last page.

iUniverse rev. date: 10/28/2019

For my children: Owen, Ian, and Anna-Reese.

As you travel through life, always know that I am not far away. I hope my memoir inspires you to stay strong and keep pushing through life's storms.

CONTENTS

Contents

AUTHOR'S NOTE

This book is a nonfiction memoir centering on a personal health battle and a story of triumph over tragedy. The people, places, and events are all real.

ACKNOWLEDGMENTS

Special thanks to the countless people who have had a hand in my diagnosis, treatment, and recovery during this long health battle, including my husband, Brandon Thomas; my parents, Johnny and Sherry Manis; my children, Owen, Ian, and Anna-Reese Thomas; countless friends and family who have been right by my side; The staff at St. Francis Hospital in Memphis, Tennessee, Dr. Michael Muhlert, St. Francis Hospital, Memphis Tennessee, Columbia Doctors from New York, Dr. Lawrence Lenke, Surgeon in Chief at New York Presbyterian Hospital in New York, the staff at New York Presbyterian Hospital; New York, Dr. Stephen Gipson with Spine Specialty Center in Memphis, Tennessee; Baptist Rehabilitation, and Integrative Physical Therapy, and DeSoto Athletic Club. The Brill Family New York, Donna Hartsoe, Christy Hardin Williams, and The Ramsey Family Memphis, Tennessee.

CHAPTER 1

Bright Beginnings

I have often said that I'm one big collection of the people I have met. Sometimes life turns out the way you want, and sometimes it doesn't. When it doesn't, you have to turn the tears and pain into something meaningful. In the hard times, you have to remember today is beautiful. At that moment, your focus might just shift directions. Just when you think your life is ending, it is actually beginning. Maybe you have been assigned this enormous mountain to show others that it can be moved. Take that enormous jump and hope you don't feel the fall.

When I was a little girl, I dreamed of living in a big castle that was painted pink and sprinkled with gold glitter and rhinestones everywhere. There would be a window in front, and I wanted a big, fancy chandelier people could see from miles away. That was the dream I had. After all, every little girl has to dream big, right?

Our family was a typical middle-class family. We never wanted for anything and never lacked much of anything special. We always ate dinner together. My mother always cooked a good home-cooked meal, and we always talked about our days.

Little did I know that one thing added into our conversation at the family dinner table one evening would later come in handy. Whatever we discussed, my parents never failed to tell my sister and I how proud they were of us. Before I knew it, I was in the third grade. My older sister Jenny was involved in an extracurricular activity: cheerleading. My parents hired a coach to get her ready for her first set of cheerleading tryouts.

Sometimes the coach would come to our house, but as a rule, we would go to Southaven High School, where my sister would practice for hours on the high school auditorium stage and sometimes in the gymnasium, where tryouts were held. She would practice for what seemed like an eternity but in actuality it was only a few hours. When it was time for tryouts, my sister was more than ready.

I can't recall what outfit she wore, but I remember my mother checking my sister and I out early to get her ready. My big sister looked cute, and even as little as I was at the time, I was just as excited and nervous as she was in hoping she'd make the team. Well, cheerleading tryouts came and went—and my sister made the team! My big sister was excited, as were her coach, Debbie; my parents; and myself. Not long after the tryout date, practices, games, and competitions began. I especially remember going with her to compete at the Mid-South Fair, regionals, and, of course, the most famous competition: nationals at Walt Disney World in Orlando, Florida.

My sister's team was so good that they won first place at regionals, which automatically gave them a bid to nationals. They had practiced hard and tweaked every single motion until it was perfect. They had already won first place at the fair competition, which gave them a bid to nationals which was a particular competition that cost my parents a whole lot of money—thousands of dollars with flights, coaching fees, uniforms, and more. The list goes on and on. Nationals was my first experience in going to Walt Disney World and gave me the idea, hope, and dream to one day work for Disney and the mouse himself.

That particular year, the team didn't win, but as I recall, they did a darn good job and hit every motion, stunt, pyramid, and dance routine perfectly and placed as the first runner-up. The experience at Disney was especially great for me because I got all the benefits of going to Walt Disney World, but didn't have the pressure of practicing every single minute, as my big sister and her cheer squad mates did.

By that time, I was playing softball, my only sport at that point. My dad was commissioner of the girls' Southaven Softball Association. We lived and breathed softball. My sweet mom would pick my sister and I up from school and run through a fast-food drive-through, and we would change into our uniforms in the car. On the days when my sister Jenny had cheerleading practice, she would change from cheer gear into her softball uniform. Eventually, little did I know, that would be my life as well.

As far as the softball life was concerned, we enjoyed it. My dear old dad really enjoyed it. It became a lifestyle for our family. My sister was a pitcher, and boy, could she throw a mean pitch! One time, our team lost. My dad felt my sister could have pitched a little better, so guess what? The next day, in the heat of the summer, in the front yard, Jenny had to pitch, and I had to catch her. It was a long hour of catching her fast pitches—or at least trying to. I wasn't very good. I couldn't hit the ball for anything, and I rarely got to play, but I was the team's biggest cheerleader. I would scream chants in the dugout so loudly that all of the city of Southaven could hear me. My favorite chant was "From moon to sun, the Southaven Renegades are number one!"

We practiced and practiced, and eventually, I became good. I started hitting the ball, and I would alternate two different positions on the field: second base and catcher. I loved catching and wearing all that equipment. It made me feel special, but honestly, aside from catching the ball and throwing people out, the part I really loved was being behind the batter and chanting, "Hey, batter, batter, your feet sure do smell!"

Before I knew it, my parents were getting calls from multiple coaches who wanted me on their teams for the next year. Once the next year came, I went through the draft. I was still young, but I remember two coaches going back and forth with my parents, telling them why I should be on their teams.

I ended up playing for a team called the Blues. It was a wonderful experience with a great coach. I became good friends with the coach's daughter. After all, we shared the same name. She was sweet to me and always made me feel special. I spent the night with her often, and those days always have been cherished memories for sure. I still see the coach of that team from time to time, and he always gives me the warmest, most genuine hug.

Time went on, and I was in the sixth grade. I played softball and was a tomboy. I loved snakes and playing in the dirt, and I got into dirt bike racing, a type of racing in which you ride your bike as fast as you can around a big dirt track. In one race, I won second place. There were only two kids in the division, including me, but hey, I placed! Let's just say I was not a girlie girl. I did not like bows, dresses, or any girl colors. Now, years later, that is definitely not the case. I love anything pretty. I love the color pink, flowers, rhinestones, high heels, and lots of makeup, especially lip gloss that sparkles.

By that time, I was near the end of my sixth-grade school year and about to enter junior high school. One night at dinner, my mom said, "Hey, Nik, guess what?"

I said, "What, Mom?"

She said, "You are going to try out for cheerleading! I signed you up today."

I looked at her as if she had lost her ever-loving mind and said, "Do what?"

She repeated herself. "You're going to try out for junior high cheerleader, and I got you the cutest outfit to wear."

"And just what does this cute outfit look like?" I asked.

She said, "It's a pink-and-purple striped shirt with pink shorts, and you're going to wear your hair in pigtails with big pink bows!"

I was in shock. I looked around, thinking maybe a friend, neighbor, or relative was there, and she was speaking to someone else.

She said, "Nikki, are you listening to me?"

I said, "Yes, Mother, I heard you, and I am not trying out for no cheerleading squad. I like dirt and softball and playing with snakes. Besides, I do not like the color pink!"

We went back and forth for what seemed like forever at the time. Needless to say, I lost the argument and knew I had to try out for the cheerleading squad. Somehow, I was alright with it because I knew I was horrible and not the cutesy cheerleading type. I didn't understand the concept behind sharp motions and sticking to the eight-count routine. When my mother would make me practice at night, I'd whisper to my dad, "Help me, please!"

My dear dad would just shrug and say, "You'll be fine."

I was not happy about this decision at all. Lots of my friends were trying out, and all the talk at the lunch table at school was about cheerleading. My best friend, Christina, was trying out. I knew she would make the team because she was pretty and tall, with long legs, and could cheer and dance like nobody's business, but that just wasn't me. I knew I was horrible and would never make the team with my tomboy looks, terrible gymnastics and motions, and overall bad cheerleading ability.

Cheerleading tryout day arrived. I knew I would never make the team but had to get through the tryouts just to appease my mother. After all, my sweet mother had cheered back in the day, so naturally, she wanted her daughters to follow in her footsteps.

I was one of the last to try out. I wore the ridiculous pink-and-purple outfit and had my hair in pigtails with the big bows attached.

The tryouts were an all-day affair. Everyone had a number and tried out with motions, gymnastics, and a cheer and dance learned at the pre-tryout cheer clinic. After everyone tried out, we all had to get into a big circle on the gymnasium floor. The cheer sponsor announced, "We have selected our cheerleading team for the new school year, and if we call your number out, you will come to the front."

I thought, *Just great. I won't make it, and I'll be left by myself on the gym floor with everyone staring at me.* I could envision it all—everyone pointing and laughing loudly while saying, "You didn't make it." I can remember the feeling as if it were yesterday.

The sponsor started calling out the numbers, and I was the last number called. I nervously thought, *They'll never call my number out*, but they did!

"Number twenty-five!"

Everyone started cheering and hollering for me. "Way to go, Nikki!"

That moment, my feelings about cheerleading

changed. I felt a sense of accomplishment that was outstanding. I will never forget the feeling I felt that day as long as I live. I was talked into doing something I didn't think I could do and didn't want to do. Come to find out I was indeed horrible, but they thought I was a good fit that they just had to put me on the team. I'm sure their decision had nothing to do with the fact that my older sister was already a cheerleader and well established in the cheer community.

All I knew was that I had made cheerleader, even if I was the last one, and would give it everything I had. I might not have been the best, but I would do my best. I realized that doing your best, which is all you can do, is the best feeling in the world.

We started practicing right away. I was still in sixth grade, so we would take the school bus over to the junior high for practice every day after school. We would start by stretching our legs and arms. Holding those splits was my least favorite part. Little did I know that holding splits stretches your legs enough to start preparing you for toe touches. A toe touch is a jump in which you split your legs and go as high as you can in the air.

We would then start practicing motions, jumps, chants, and cheers for games and dance routines for the first big thing we would do as a team: cheerleading camp. Cheerleading camp was around the middle of June, so once school was out for the summer, we would practice twice a day to get ready. As I prepared, in my mind, I knew this would be a learning curve for me. The practices were tough, but so was I, and that gave me somewhat of an edge over a few others. I was always being told things to improve on, so I would.

I was little, so I figured they would use me as a flyer but not at first. I was a spotter, so I helped the others in the back and protected the ones who were holding the girls up. Those girls were known as bases, and of course, the flyers were the ones on top. I didn't mind that position much because I was always willing to help others, even as a small child. My daddy told me, "Be a help to others, and be nice to everyone you meet. You always want to be known as a nice person."

It was finally time for cheerleading camp. We were going to Memphis, Tennessee, for the cheerleading camp, which was held by the Universal Cheerleaders Association.

Everyone brought many decorations, such as posters, balloons, and streamers, to decorate their door. It was practice, practice, practice from there on out. We stayed in the dorms on the University of Memphis campus, but we spent little time in those dorm rooms. On our first day, they blared lots of great music from the loudspeakers, and we had a huge rally with cheerleading squads from all over. I still remember that one of the songs played was "Cool" by Morris Day and the Time. To this day, every time I hear that song, it reminds me of my first cheer camp experience. It all comes right back as if it were yesterday.

We went through the week, learning brand-new material and competing at night with other squads for ribbons and various awards that would be given out on the last day. It was kind of nerve-racking for me; I hoped I would remember all the cheers, chants, and eight-counts of the routines we had practiced over and over. I watched the Universal Cheerleading Association members flip all over the place and throw girls up so high in basket tosses that it seemed as if they reached the sky! As cheerleading camp came to a close, it was filled with music, stunts, and cheerleading routines.

Awards were called out, and we all ran up together as a squad to receive them. Overall, I had a great experience at my first cheerleading camp. After the camp members dismissed us, we went up to our dorm rooms one final time to pack and take down the decorations. We shared lots of memories, laughter, and friendships made to last a lifetime.

We still had quite a bit of the summer left before the new school year began. In between cheerleading practice and softball games, I spent time hanging out with friends, going to movies, and swimming. Of course, at night, I would practice with an older cheerleader to get extra help when needed, and my sister would help as well.

I would do sit-ups and sit in the splits for thirty minutes at a time to help with lengthening my legs for toe touches. This was a difficult task as I would find out later that my legs are different lengths. I also found that using our large TV in the living room to lift myself into the air with splits helped with toe-touch jumps tremendously. I was bound and determined to be better than I had been at camp and to come back improved.

School started, and I was in the seventh grade. It was

a great feeling to be one of the cool kids and on the cheerleading squad. After school every day, we would practice for a couple hours. Once it got cooler outside, we moved our practices to the gym. I had improved so much that now I got to be a flyer, which was very cool.

The feeling of being on top and flying in the air was awesome. Besides, everyone watches the flyers. I stayed as tight as I could so the bases wouldn't drop me. We would cheer for the football games at night, and soon it would be time for our first cheerleading competition: the Mid-South Fair in Memphis, Tennessee.

It drew near September, and it was time for the fair competition. It was usually outside at the fairgrounds. They called our squad name: "It's the Chargers from Southaven, Mississippi!" We ran out together, got in place as quickly and tightly as we could, and waited for the cheerleading captain to say, "Ready? Okay!"

The cheer portion began, followed by the dance routine we'd practiced so perfectly for. After we were done, we all yelled, "Go Chargers!" Our squad then patiently waited for the other squads to perform and compete. If your squad was announced at the end, you were headed to regionals.

Intense practices and the regionals came and went. We started cheering for basketball games, and before I knew it, my seventh-grade year was over, and it was time for cheerleading tryouts all over again. I couldn't believe it. Something I'd been kind of forced to do had turned into something I dearly loved, and I wanted to get better and better.

Cheerleading tryouts for my eighth-grade year came and went, and I made the squad. That year was going to be special—I just knew it. My math teacher, Ms. Thompson, became our cheerleading sponsor. One morning, my mom told me that we had to have the house super clean because Ms. Thompson was coming over. I thought it was strange that she was coming over but thought they were just going to talk about cheerleading. That day, I got some exciting news: I was to be named co-captain of the cheerleading squad! The captain was my best friend, Christina. I was happy. I felt honored. All that extra practicing had paid off in the biggest way possible.

It was a great year of cheering and playing softball, and I had a special title that I had worked hard for but hadn't expected. I just wanted to get better at cheerleading and improve my skills; I hadn't known it would lead to my being co-captain of the entire cheerleading squad. My eighth-grade year went pretty much how the year before had gone but much better. Then it was time to pull out the big guns, so to speak. It was time for me to try out for high school cheerleader. Time flew by so quickly that it felt unreal at times. My mother checked me out of school early so I could come home and get ready for tryouts. My outfit, hair, makeup, and moves were perfect, and I was ready.

I tried my hardest, running out and doing a round-off back handspring. I stood in the middle of the gym floor, hitting every motion and yelling every word. Then it was time for my dance routine. I tried out to a song by Huey Lewis and the News. That was my favorite part.

The results were in: I had officially been given a spot on the Southaven varsity cheerleading squad. That year, my older sister Jenny and I would get to cheer together. It was particularly nerve-racking because now that I was on the varsity team, I knew I had better be up for the challenge because there was some really great talent on that squad. Just as in the previous years, we started practicing to get ready for camp, competitions, and the new school year.

Even though cheerleaders typically were pretty popular among the student body, I was always scared of rejection. At the start of every school day, I didn't hang out in the commons area, as most of the other cheerleaders and football players did. I would put my things away in my locker and head straight to class.

Having my sister and I on the same cheerleading squad put extra pressure on my parents. At one point, my father worked a couple extra jobs to help pay for it all. Being a cheerleader comes with a hefty price tag. We seemed to make it just fine. It was a busy life: cheerleader by day and softball player by night. Many days, we would change in the car, have late dinners, do our homework, crash by the end of the night, and then get up and do it all over again.

Soon it would be time for nationals in Orlando, Florida, and we would all go as a family. We had moved by that time to a home that had a swimming pool. It was fun to live at a house with a pool. In the summer, many of our friends came over to swim, including after cheer practices and softball games. Since I was a big high schooler by then, there were parties on the weekends. My sister was quite the popular one and always was getting ready to go to some party or out with friends. I, however, never did.

CHAPTER 2

The Rise and Fall

I would swim and visit with friends throughout the day, but when it came to going to parties and such, I always stayed home. I was frightened of the thought of talking to people at parties, and the thought of someone walking away for a minute left me with fear, so I preferred to stay home and watch Friday night videos. It was 1989. It would be a pivotal year for many reasons. I was now in the tenth grade, and my sister was a senior in high school. We were both on the varsity cheer squad again, but since my sister was a senior, it would be the last year we would cheer together. We were a busy family.

Cheerleading became our life. One particular warm spring day, we were practicing outside in front of the high school, working on a three-man-high pyramid. I was to be on the top. I heard, "Five, six, seven, eight," and I took a deep breath and dipped down to be lifted up. I

15

made it all the way to the top. I stood as tightly as I could, and then, all of a sudden, the world stopped: I fell all the way to the ground. My breath got knocked out of me. I couldn't breathe. I couldn't speak. The cheerleaders and others gathered around. My parents were called to come get me. They were told, "Nikki is hurt; she fell off the pyramid."

Eventually, my breath came back as I came to. I slowly sat up as my parents arrived, and I went home to rest. Before long, the inevitable back pain began, and it lasted all through the night. By morning, I was in so much pain that my parents took me to see an orthopedic doctor and surgeon. He was nice and took good care of me. They could all see the horrible pain I was in. The doctor examined me from head to toe. I had an x-ray done. We waited patiently on the doctor, not imagining the news we would soon hear. The words we were going to hear would forever be etched in my mind, and little did I know that would be the moment when God said, "Here it comes, sweet girl. It's going to be tough, but so are you, and I'll be right by your side every step of the way."

We heard the words for the first time: "She's got a fracture in her spine, and she's got Scoliosis." The worst part followed: "She needs surgery."

I stood there with the room spinning. My parents were in shock. My mom and dad asked the doctor, "What does this mean? How will this affect her?"

My immediate thought was *Forget all that mumbo jumbo. What does this mean for my cheerleading career from here moving forward? I've worked so hard. I can't stop now, but at the same time, I am in horrible pain. Absolute horrible pain. But surgery? Surgery!*

My parents and I left with information, records, and the results of my x-ray scan in case we wanted to seek a second opinion. We drove home. It seemed like a long drive, especially since we were all silent. No radio, no talking—nothing. My parents were scared, and frankly, so was I. Now that I understand what Scoliosis was—a curvature of the spine—The seriousness of this injury and the pain I was feeling all started to make sense.

We talked in great detail the next day. My mother said, "You know, Nikki, we are ultimately leaving this up to you, but we think you should do the surgery. It's the only way the Scoliosis can be corrected."

Without thinking, I immediately said, "Nope, nope, nope. I am not having this surgery, because that would be the end for me as far as my cheerleading career is concerned, and I have worked so very hard."

My parents looked at me in shock.

I said, "Mom and Dad, I could get cheerleading scholarships. I could really go places with cheerleading. If I have this surgery, there's no more gymnastics, no more pyramids, and no more cheerleading for me. I will be toast. This is the only talent I have, and I can't let it end like this."

My father stayed strong, as he always does. My mother didn't cry, but we both had huge tears welling up in our eyes. My mother, being a nurse, knew what the diagnosis of Scoliosis meant for the rest of my life health wise, but I didn't, not at that point anyway.

So the decision was made: I would not be having the surgery. We would go back to the doctor toward the end of the week to discuss our options.

When we went back for the follow-up appointment, the doctor asked, "What did you all decide?"

I spoke up and said, "I decided I am not having the surgery."

The doctor said, "Well, we need to talk about nonsurgical options. You are going to be fitted for a back brace."

A week later, the horrible back brace arrived. It was big and bulky and made of hard, thick fiberglass. It had a metal bar that went around my neck, down the front of my sternum, and down my back the length of my entire spine. The brace was the worst thing ever.

It was not only uncomfortable but actually hurt. It compressed my spine and sternum so tightly that I could barely breathe. Night after night, my parents would strap me in, and all I could do was cry and beg, saying, "Please don't make me wear this." I would cry myself to sleep every single night, thinking, *This can't be real. This can't be happening, and I cannot wear this for the rest of my life.*

I continued to wear the brace for the next year. My parents always told me to stand up straight whenever they saw me. It physically hurt to stand up straight. They also watched me walk back and forth, and there was a strange popping noise coming from my back. It was prevalent. I could not only hear it but also feel it. We all just thought it was part of the Scoliosis and an effect of wearing the brace.

I asked often to remove the brace, and my parents could see the physical and emotional pain it was causing, so they finally obliged and allowed me to quit wearing the brace. It was a strange feeling. I felt a sense of relief that I no longer had to wear the brace, but I was also a bit sad, as I knew deep down that the Scoliosis was not just going to heal on its own. Little did I know that embarrassing, crude questions would soon start to come.

Regarding the curvature of my spine, the way I stood and walked, and just my overall look in general, I had no idea people could be so cruel and not think about their words before they opened their mouths. I got questions like "What's wrong with your back?" and "Why are you so hunched over?" Tears would form but only internally instead of externally. I hid much from many, especially the way I was truly feeling inside. It was unnerving. If I asked people questions and reacted the way some did, I would feel horrible, but as a rule, people just don't think. I would always explain as nicely as I could about the cheerleading accident, the fall, and my spine condition, Scoliosis, which would continue to progress.

I finished out the year barely with my back brace, pain and all. I kept moving forward with life and tried out for cheerleading again the next year, my junior year. I was still in pain, but I got used to it. I tried carrying on with life as normally as I could with cheer and hanging out with friends. I was still flying on top of those pyramids and taking gymnastics. The one thing I wanted more than anything was to flip all over the place. The best I could do was a round-off series with only two back handsprings. I knew that was all I could do. It made me sad to watch others; it seemed incredibly easy for them. For me, though, it wasn't possible due to my spine.

It took everything out of me to throw one back handspring, let alone a few more. Since I had a lack of gymnastic ability, I would overcompensate with tight motions, dance, and climbing to the top of stunts or pyramids. I just wanted to be the best I could be, despite my spine condition. Every time I climbed to the top of those high pyramids, I couldn't help but remember that horrible fall. I finally had to trust my bases, my spotters, and those in between. I was learning trust at a young age that would eventually come back around full circle.

I made it to my senior year of high school. Tryouts came and went, and I made the squad again. I had contemplated sitting out a year, but I then thought, *I am not a quitter. I must keep on going.* It was a year of excitement. Along with all the cheerleading activities came a lot of fun too, including senior decorating of hallways and floats for homecoming and my senior letter jacket. We always had a football player or two whom we adopted for the year, and we would leave little surprises for them in the locker room. Even though I wasn't very outgoing and never mingled in the commons area, I got to know several football players since I cheered, and I would see many when I went to the locker room. They would speak to me and say, "Hey, Nikki," left me with the hugest smile on my face.

The end of my senior year was bittersweet because I would never cheer for Southaven High School again. By that time, I had fallen in love with Arkansas State University. My father was from Arkansas, and through a summer job, I'd become friends with many who went there and always talked highly of the school. My parents thought it was best that I go to a junior college first. I tried out for the Northwest cheerleading squad, my first coed squad. I not only made the team but also received a full-ride cheerleading scholarship. What a wonderful feeling that was!

I had another cheerleading injury that year. We were stunting. My stunt partner and I fell sideways, and I landed on my right ankle. My back was spared that time, but my ankle was not. It was shattered, and I found myself having total reconstructive ankle surgery. I am not sure which was worse: the falling on the ankle or the surgery itself.

I healed from that, and my first and only year of junior college came to a close. It was finally time for me to go to my dream college: Arkansas State University.

I remember my mom standing in the kitchen crying because I was officially moving out and going to real college. I tried to console her the best I could. My parents and I made it to Jonesboro, Arkansas, the home of Arkansas State University. I met my new college roommate and got moved into the dorm. I felt immediately I had picked the perfect college. Most everyone I'd gone to school with back home had gone to local colleges, such as the University of Mississippi, Memphis State University, and Mississippi State University. I was ready. I wanted to go away to a school that was just far enough away from home but just close enough that I could come home on the weekends if I wanted to.

A few weeks passed by, and it was time to try out for cheerleader. Of course, I would make the squad, or I sure thought I would any way. It just made sense. That was what I had worked so incredibly hard for and dreamed of.

Tryout day arrived, and I prepped for tryouts, as I had always done. I had a cute outfit and new tennis shoes, and my hair and makeup were perfectly in place. I remembered every motion of the cheer and dance taught at the clinic the week prior. I gave it my best shot.

For the first time in my life, I did not make the squad! I thought, *What? How could this be?* I had never not made a cheerleading squad. I didn't understand. *What did I do wrong?* I waited until everyone was gone except the cheer sponsor, and I approached her and asked, "Can I ask you a question?"

She replied, "Sure you can."

I said, "As you're aware, I didn't make the team. Can you tell me why?"

She said, "Believe me, we were just as shocked as you are. You're very cute, you have the look, and you hit everything perfectly, but it was the gymnastics that held you back and kept you off the squad."

I just nodded and explained, "My spine condition keeps me from tumbling like the rest." I went through the whole entire story of how I fell, the fractured spine, back brace, and all of that.

She gave me a dumbfounded, shocked look and said, "My goodness, how are you still cheering after all that?" She then said, "I know how much you wanted to make the squad, because I can see it in your face."

CHAPTER 3

Dance and Disney

"Based on what you've just told me about your spine, I don't think your tumbling skills will ever get to the point that we are looking for," she said. "You should try out for the dance team."

I was sad about not making the squad, but I picked myself up, as I had always done before, and tried out for the dance team, which was known as the A-Team. I made the dance team.

Dance was totally different from cheerleading, with no gymnastics, tumbling, cheering, or pyramids. We went to a dance camp and a few competitions, but our primary responsibility was to perform at basketball games during halftime. We learned a routine to the song from the movie *Speed Racer*. A few of the dance team members said, "Wouldn't it be great if we had some cool props?"

It just so happened that I was coming home that weekend, and we had a fast food restaurant named Checkers. I went inside, explained who I was, told them about our routine, and then asked, "Can we borrow the two big flags out front?" One was black and one was red both were checkerboard print.

The manager replied, "Sure!"

Monday of the following week, I said, "Guess what, everyone? I got us some really cool props for our routine." I ran out to my car and brought in the flags.

Everyone laughed and said, "Nikki, how in the world did you pull this off?" I explained that I just went into Checkers and asked. They thought it was great. The flags would go with our song. It gave me a great feeling to have voluntarily done something that the others never asked me to do, but deep inside I knew they greatly appreciated my efforts.

That was a great routine. We used the flags, and I returned them a few weeks later. Helping others has always given me so much joy. It's a feeling I can't explain. I am a helper and have a big heart.

I pressed on for my freshman year of college. I went through the sorority process and became a member of the AOII sorority. I loved Arkansas State University. I was meeting lots of people and doing well.

Being in a sorority meant I got to go to parties, swaps, and mixers. There was a huge pageant held every year by the Greek members called Miss Greek Pledge. I found out that another fraternity had selected me to compete in the Miss Greek Pledge pageant. I had to have a dress, swimsuit, costume, and talent.

When it was time for the annual pageant, I was ready. My dress was royal blue and gold. I borrowed a swimsuit from another girl who had done the pageant the previous year. This pageant had a lot to do with a funny talent—the funnier the better. I portrayed a famous singer. I had the outfit, the wig, and the music. I had the routine down to a science.

As luck would have it, I won the pageant. I thought they had made a mistake, until everyone was saying, "Nikki, that's you! You're the winner!"

My mother, my sister, and my sister's boyfriend at the time made the long drive down to watch me compete. I had never competed in a pageant in my older years, so being crowned as winner gave me a feeling I'll never forget. At that moment, I knew that despite my condition, my poor posture, the pain, and my failures that had come and gone and the ones I would have throughout the rest of my life, God truly had some special plans for me.

The next day, while walking on campus, I had many people I had never met come up to me to congratulate me. Even though I had only won a school pageant for the first time ever, I felt like Miss America!

My college years went on, and I continued to be on the dance team. During that time, I came home from college one weekend to audition for a job. I had a dream to one day work for Disney. I didn't care what the job was, but I thought, *Wouldn't it be great if I could be one of those characters?* I didn't tell anyone, not even my parents, because I knew they would tell everyone they knew that I was to audition for Disney, and if I didn't make the cut, everyone would know. To prepare for the audition, I was connected with a coach. He told me to get into ballet immediately, so that was what I did. I took a full summer at the best school: Memphis Concert Ballet.

As my luck would have it, I made it. I was officially named a cast member for Walt Disney World! Working for Disney was a wonderful experience. There were parades, parties, and lots of autograph signing. Signing autographs was the best part. I thought, *How great it is that all these boys and girls come from all over the world so I can sign their autograph book! Pretty remarkable*. Because of that job, I knew I wanted to work with children and be a role model for children. In knowing that, I knew what my career would be: I would become an elementary school teacher.

At the end of that year, I went back for my final year in college and got my degree from Arkansas State University. Shortly after that, I got a second degree in education. I was a board-certified educator. I was truly blessed that I achieved not only one degree but two.

During that time, I met a guy at the Peabody in Memphis who would later become my husband. When you meet your future husband, many thoughts enter your mind. *Is he really the one? Are we truly soulmates?* It's often been said that God has a reason for everything. He has your life planned out from the beginning. The Bible states "For these are the plans I have for you." There was a much bigger purpose and reason that I met my future husband that night. God had my entire life planned out, and he knew that even though I had been ridiculously blessed with many opportunities, there would come a day when I would truly have to walk through the fire. God knew to place Brandon in my life because no other man would be able to handle, endure, and withstand what he would one day have to.

College graduations, cheerleading, dance, and Disney transcended state lines from Mississippi to Florida, to Arkansas into teaching jobs and marriage. We were married at the most beautiful Catholic church in Memphis, Tennessee. It is actually a Cathedral and the only one in Memphis. I once attended a wedding there and knew that's where I wanted to get married. After the wedding, I was blessed enough to get my first teaching job and taught for five years in a private school setting. I loved it. While teaching in the private school setting, I was blessed with one of the highest honors a teacher can receive: I was selected as Teacher of the Year. I felt proud and humbled. I truly had some of the best students and parents ever, many of whom I'll never forget. I had set a goal to be the best teacher I knew and was determined to inspire, create, and change lives one child at a time.

While I was pregnant with one of my children, I became close with many of the teachers there. One asked me, "So when will you return from maternity leave?"

I said, "You know, I think I'll come back for sure by October because I absolutely love teaching that month, with all of the fall activities."

My class of students became like my own children.

I loved them all. When you are a teacher, you aren't just a teacher. You are a teacher, nurse, parent, and friend all at the same time. I was always finding ways to decorate my classroom or create learning activities with my students.

My favorite part about teaching was center time, or learning stations, a time when students would rotate throughout the room. I would use that time to visit with each student and ask him or her about the weekend or something he or she was excited about. Most importantly, I would teach them how to read and enjoy reading. It was an opportunity to sit and rest as well. My back pain crept up from time to time, but I knew I had to keep going. After all, I was now married and had a baby, so I had no time between teaching and raising my babies. We had a nice little surprise after baby number one entered the world. I became pregnant with baby number two. It was another little boy; Ian. Soon thereafter, I began teaching in the public school spectrum, so we moved back to Southaven, Mississippi.

My husband and I felt it was time to make a move so we would be closer our parents' houses, where our kids stayed for a few years. We bought our first house after living in a loft apartment. Life was great other than the occasional pain here and there. In the year 2007 something really special happened, our final addition to the family came. A little girl named Anna-Reese. I knew if I ever had a little girl, I wanted her to have a double name. My little family was now complete. I do remember with all three children, I had lots of major back pains.

It was now the year 2009. My children were healthy, growing, and happy. I always loved playing with them, chasing after them, and dressing them up. The two boys, who were thirteen months apart, were always in cute hats or caps, and of course, my daughter wore anything smocked and big bows. During the summer months, we would play, go to parks and museums, and have lots of play dates, as I had many friends with children the same ages as mine.

My parents had a built-in swimming pool, so we went swimming multiple times a week. I wanted to be the best mom I could be. I knew that some days I fell short, but I always made sure that no matter what, my children knew I loved them.

Three years passed by, and it was now 2012. When I was getting dressed, putting on makeup, or cleaning the house, such as mopping the floor, I was beginning to show signs of losing my breath, and the pain in my lower spine had progressed further. I made it for a year just by taking hot baths, using heating pads, and resting when I felt I could. By the year 2013, I knew it was time to do something drastic.

I knew I needed back surgery. I guess all the cheering, dancing, Disney performances, teaching, and childbirth finally, it had caught up with me. The search was on. I began searching for a spine surgeon. I went to see one doctor in Memphis. He examined me and said, "You have a pretty bad case of Scoliosis, and it's my thought that there's a lot of pressure; however, I don't think I can do this surgery. It would be way more complex than what I feel like I can offer you."

I left a little discouraged but knew that as big as the area we lived in was, there were plenty of other doctors I could see. I scheduled an appointment with another surgeon. He didn't have a very good bedside manner, something that's important to me. I knew this doctor was not in the cards either, so I kept searching.

During this process, I told a friend about the back pain and said I hadn't had the best luck in finding a good spine doctor to help me. She suggested a doctor who had done her friend's surgery. He came highly recommended. I immediately looked up his reviews, and they were all good. He was at St. Francis Hospital in Memphis, Tennessee.

I had a month's wait, and then it was finally time for my appointment. I was nervous and excited at the same time. I took a half day off from school so I would have plenty of time for the drive, paperwork, and all that. I showed up for the appointment. I kept waiting and waiting. I finally got called to the front desk. The front desk nurse said, "Are you Mrs. Thomas?"

I replied, "Yes, ma'am, I am."

She said, "I am so sorry, but we can't see you today."

I thought I had heard her wrong and said, "What did you say?"

She said, "There's an issue with your insurance. We don't take your insurance."

I said, "Oh yes you do. You're on the approved doctor list."

After much frustration, I left in tears. Before I got to my car, she called me to say there had been a mistake. Since I was a teacher, they'd assumed I had the standard teacher's insurance, which they didn't take. They figured out that I was on my husband's insurance, which they did take. I told her I was upset that I had taken off a half day of work. She was sorry for the misunderstanding. She assured me I would love this doctor, and they would do everything they could for me. I was tempted to throw my hands in the air and just say, "Forget it," but something inside me told me to give it one more chance.

CHAPTER 4

Spine Surgeries and Pain

It was a cold January day. It was dark and dreary outside, but I've always remembered this quote by an unknown author: "When the world says, 'Give up,' hope whispers, 'Try one more time.'"

The next day, I went back to the hospital for my appointment. I still had the same nervous but excited feeling. I wore a royal blue sweater, my favorite sweater, which I thought maybe would somehow bring me good luck with this third doctor. I had to wait and wait some more. Why is it that when you have an appointment for a certain time, you still have to wait?

The doctor came in and greeted me with a smile. He said, "Hello, Mrs. Thomas." He examined me from head to toe. I went through my entire story of the cheerleading fall and all that. It just so happened that he had a daughter who cheered, so he understood where

I was coming from. He had a great bedside manner, so I knew immediately he was the one. He would perform my spinal-fusion surgery. It was official. My spinal surgery was scheduled for Monday, April 8, 2013 by Dr. Douglas Linville. I could hardly sign all the paperwork with all the emotions running through my mind.

I drove as fast as I could to my parents' house. They had just finished dinner. I asked them if we could go into the living room, as I had something important to talk to them about.

I could see the nervous looks on their faces. I said, "Don't worry; I'm not pregnant." They both laughed loudly. With tears in my eyes, I said, "I just left St. Francis Hospital, and my spinal surgery has been scheduled for April."

Both of my parents were emotional and gave me big hugs. They said, "We knew this day would eventually come." They were right. After the years of pain, pushing through, and explaining my crooked back to so many people, I was finally getting the surgery my parents had once begged me to get.

I went home and tended to my children, and then I got on my computer and decided it was time to tell everyone.

I decided to write a blog. Little did I know, this blog would cost me later. I started from the beginning. Many already knew my entire story, but many didn't. Writing the blog was therapeutic for me. I don't know when I got more phone calls and messages: after writing and posting the first blog update or when I would become pregnant with my daughter a few years earlier. We kept my pregnancy with my daughter a secret until Christmas cards were mailed out. No one knew until they saw a Christmas card that said, "The Thomas family and baby!" Both gave me a great feeling. I felt such a sense of relief after sharing the news about the spine surgery that I couldn't explain it. I finally felt for once that all was right in the world.

Soon my spine would be fixed, and I would be pain free, or so I thought. The next four months passed by. It finally became April, and I was a few weeks away from spine surgery. I would be in the hospital for at least a week and then home for recovery. I had picked April because I knew I would have the entire summer to recover and would be good to go by the time the next school year began.

Finally, it was surgery day. I couldn't sleep the night before. I was anxious, nervous, excited, and just ready. I was up by three o'clock in the morning. We had to be at the hospital by five o'clock. The surgery was set to begin at seven. I remember yelling at my husband, "We are going to be late!"

His reply was sarcastic and funny, as usual: "They can't start without you. You're the one they are operating on, Sparkles!"

Sparkles was a nickname he used for me. He asked me once, "If you were famous and had a stage name, what would it be?"

I immediately responded, "Sparkles. Because I love anything that sparkles, as most girls do!"

We finally arrived at the hospital. I made him drop me off at the front door so I could get checked in. After I checked in, they sent me to the surgery floor to start getting prepped for surgery.

Shortly after that, my husband, my mom and dad, a few of my closest friends, and my sister Mary Jane were all there for the big day. The nurse came in and said, "We are ready for you, Mrs. Thomas."

I kissed and hugged everyone. It was to be an eight- to ten-hour surgery. My husband came with me to greet my doctor before they wheeled me back. It was time, and the man of the hour had arrived: my spine surgeon. My husband had my phone, and by the time the doctor arrived, I wanted a photo because, well, I like to document everything. I was so nervous I couldn't remember the code to get into my phone at first. We got the photo, and my husband kissed me goodbye. The last thing I remember is being wheeled into surgery.

I woke up from surgery many hours later. I was back in my hospital room with all my family and friends there. I heard my mom say, "Nikki, sweetheart, Mom's here."

I immediately started crying, overcome by all the emotions I was feeling and the most intense pain I had ever felt. All I could say was "Help me; I'm hurting so badly." They had me up that night standing, but I was only able to take a few steps. The pain was unreal. I remember I was given some orange juice and immediately started vomiting and asked for a fan due to the nausea that was setting in and I became very hot. I continued on the rest of the week in the hospital, walking and doing physical therapy, and they pushed liquids and food, but I had little desire to eat due to the nausea and weakness.

My doctor came and made rounds to check on my progress daily. After being discharged from the hospital, I knew it would be a long recovery for the rest of the summer.

One week postop, I went to the doctor for a checkup. My sister drove me, and when we got to the hospital, of course, I was barely walking, taking baby steps. A nurse asked if I wanted a wheelchair. I immediately said, "Yes!"

Once it was time for me to go back to see my doctor, he wasn't thrilled to see me in a wheelchair. He wanted me walking. Being a people pleaser, I said a million times that I was sorry, but I really did need the wheelchair, even though they wanted me walking. I think seeing the patient walking somehow makes them think, *Wow, look at my patient! She's walking after one week!* He examined my incision and how I was doing. Then I had to deliver the bad news to the doctor that the meds weren't working at all. I was in horrible pain, barely able to rest from the pain. As much as I hated to ask for stronger pain medication, I knew I had to get some relief.

At that point, he could see in my eyes that I was indeed really in pain. He told me, "I'm going to get you to see my partner, who handles pain management, in just a few minutes to see if we can get you some relief." His name was Dr. Stephen Gipson. He was nice and caring. We connected instantly. Dr. Gipson is a colorful man with a colorful history. He is a native Arkansan who studied medicine in the charter class of St. George's

University, where he did his clinical rotations, in the south of England. His personality grew more flamboyant from all the different communities in which he studied. His office is resplendent with pictures of aircraft, as he is a pilot and a World War II history nut.

He said he had been one of only three doctors in Memphis who treated chronic-pain patients when he started practice in 1984. By the time I saw him, he was a seasoned and skilled doctor with many years' experience, which I called upon regularly. He talked of his varying interests and, of course, his children frequently. I was to find that I would become close to him and dependent on his guidance for many years to come. He put me on Oxycontin. This particular medicine is a longer-acting one. It would release throughout the day, lasting longer. I now had the short-acting medicine Percocet and the long-acting Oxycontin. I thought, *Isn't this the medicine that's all the buzz right now?* I had only heard of it through the news.

Dr. Gipson thoroughly explained how the medicine would work. I would alternate the two, and if I had any problems, I was to call the office, and he would get me right back in. I was on my way.

My sister and I were able to get the prescriptions filled while we were at the hospital. Once we arrived back at my house, she was able to get me settled. For the most part, the two medicines in combination helped me find relief from pain and get the rest I needed to begin recovery.

A few weeks passed. I felt sick and bloated and much

pressure. A major side effect of the pain medicine was constipation. Pain medicine acts as a numbing agent in your entire system and paralyzes your colon.

Two weeks went by, and my colon was inflamed and severely impacted. I couldn't pass any stool, no matter what I tried. That, of course, put extra pressure on my lower spine. I was crying and hurting, and my husband didn't know what to do to help me. I think that for the most part, men want to just fix things, and this time, he couldn't. I felt my intestines were starting to shut down. My mother had to come intervene. If that didn't work, then we all knew I would have no choice but to go to the hospital. By the grace of God, it worked. I was finally able to pass the stool. I felt as if I had given birth. I was relieved to have the pressure off my lower spine, and the bloated stomach pains subsided.

After that ordeal, I knew I couldn't continue with the Oxycontin. Once I did some research on that particular medicine, I found out it was notorious for backing up your bowels, and I couldn't deal with that again. I called Dr. Gipson and got in the office and told him what had happened. He then changed up some of my meds and put me on a medicine to help.

Things started to get a little better. I didn't have any more major constipation flare-ups, or at least none as bad as the one that day. The pain started to get better. I worked hard. I did lots of physical therapy, and I was running. I actually started to train for my first race.

I was able to recover enough to start the new school year. I didn't know it then, but I rushed my recovery a bit to be able to start the new school year. The school year started, and I took it as easy as I could, still doing physical therapy a couple times a week after the school day finished. I ran in my first race that same year. It was a half marathon for St. Jude. I did it with a friend of mine. I had never trained for anything like that, but I was proud of the work I had put in to get better. The race came and went. I didn't walk home with any medals but didn't come in last either, so I considered that a win. Overall, I was doing well.

I was able to get off medication, except for an occasional Tylenol. I did great for the first year and a half. My spine was straight, I had minimal pain, my breathing was better, and I was working out and running. However, a short time after the first six-month postop, I started having pelvic pain only on my left side. When I mentioned that to my spine surgeon, he immediately said, "That sounds like a female issue, and you need to see your gynecologist."

I made an appointment with that doctor. He did an ultrasound, and it showed cysts on my ovaries. He told me, "You need a hysterectomy."

I was in shock. I thought, *What? Another surgery?* I had some serious thinking to do about this. After all, it had only been six months since my last surgery.

I wanted to be free of pain, but another major surgery? I went back multiple times to my gynecologist, and we went back and forth about whether or not to take all of my reproductive organs. I was not a fan of him taking all of them. My doctor kept insisting that if I didn't have my ovaries taken out with the other organs, I would be back the next year because the cysts would affect my other organs that would've remained. I didn't know what to do because I knew that if I took out everything, there would be no turning back, and it would put me right into menopause.

My doctor put a lot of pressure on me to take everything, so naturally, that was what I did. The surgery was not laparoscopic; I was cut on my abdomen from left to right. I was in the hospital for a week.

Once I got home, I didn't feel right. Things were just not right. My body basically went into a tailspin. My hormones were raging, insomnia set in, and hot flashes began. I kept having to go back to my doctor who had done the hysterectomy, because I wasn't getting control of the hot flashes, and after a month, the pain had come back full force. My doctor more or less threw his hands in the air and said, "Well, I've done all I can do. You may have scar tissue that has formed that needs to come out."

I was in shock. I looked up and said, "What? So soon?"

He responded, "Yes, that soon." He set me up with a general surgeon who would remove the scar tissue. I went in to meet with the doctor and had all my ducks in a row, so to speak. I had radiology scans and doctor reports. I was so desperate to be free of pain that I just wanted the next surgery to be quick and over with as soon as possible. I finally was able to get in to see the general surgeon, and he agreed that I had scar tissue, and he also found I had a hernia to repair.

By that time, it was 2015. I finished my last school year after teaching for fifteen years. It was bittersweet. I knew

I had done my job. I'd taught, inspired, and formed many relationships with thousands of children and parents, but it was time for a change. I was able to get another job in the education field, just not in the classroom. It was my dream job, or so I thought. It was unfortunate timing that right before I took the new job, I had to have a surgical procedure, but I knew it would all work out.

I had the procedure in early June. Once the surgeons got in, they found another hernia. Due to the unexpected additional hernia, along with a fever after the surgery, they decided to keep me overnight for observation.

When I went home, I was in quite a bit of pain. The pain would shoot down my abdominal region, and it was excruciating. I kept thinking, *Oh my goodness, how am I going to start a new job in a few weeks?* I knew that no matter what, I would push through because I'd worked hard to get that new dream job and certainly wasn't going to lose it now.

A few weeks went by, and the pain eased up. I was doing well. I started my new job, and it was an exciting time for me.

I was only at my job a couple months. Things were going great, and then all of the sudden, I felt pain in my pelvis that radiated down to my left leg. At first, I thought it was in my head. I would actually say to myself, "Am I really in pain?" This lasted for several weeks. It finally got to the point that I woke up one morning and knew something wasn't right. Somehow, I just knew.

The pain progressed and got worse as the days went on. I went back to see the general surgeon, and he felt he had done all he could do. I thought, *How do I really know he did what he was supposed to do? Did he really remove the scar tissue? Did he really remove the hernias?* A patient is not awake during surgeries to make sure the doctors are doing their jobs. The patient also doesn't have a representative to make sure everything is going according to plan. You just have to trust that the doctors are doing the right thing. I was upset that he more or less washed his hands of my case and was done.

He at least could have referred me to someone who could help me. I thought, *Now what? Who do I go see now?* I suddenly knew this was going to be a long and drawn-out ordeal. Back to the drawing board I went. I went back to see my gynecologist. He then referred me to another known specialist in gynecology to see what could be done about the increasing pelvic pain. After many scans and tests, it was determined that my problem was not female related, and therefore, nothing could be done.

It was difficult. Because my ovaries and uterus were gone, there was nothing that could be done on that end. It started to become frustrating for me. I was in excruciating pain and running into dead end after dead end. I went to see an interventional radiologist through a mutual friend who got me a special after-hours appointment. I took everything I had: doctors' notes, operative reports, and radiology scans. He looked at my spine and said, "Based on what I have seen, it looks like you need to go back to your spine surgeon. Something could possibly be going on with your hardware."

I was grateful for the opportunity to have him look at me, but it was another dead end. I knew the next step was to go see my spine surgeon.

The following week, I had an appointment. During my spine doctor appointment, I was told that oftentimes, your hardware can give out and cause compression. Hearing this news was a bit overwhelming, but I just wanted relief and was willing to do whatever it took. My spine surgeon set up a series of radiology scans so he could get a better understanding of what might be going on. This took several weeks and several appointments. I had to get one scan done, wait for the results, and then go in to see the doctor. When nothing showed on that scan, I went for another set of imaging, waited on the results, and then went back to the doctor again.

Eventually, a second spine-revision surgery was scheduled for July 2016. Even though there was not a definite pain source, surgery was scheduled, and we were hoping for the best possible outcome. During that time, I was constantly researching failed hardware, failed spinal fusions, compression of hardware, pelvic pain, and spine pain. Furthermore, now I had pain in my left leg, so there was that to research too. There was a plethora of information out there. I read, educated myself, and researched every spare moment I had and every night before falling asleep.

Insomnia had set in, which is a major side effect of having a hysterectomy. There was a whole lot of information I had failed to receive regarding the hysterectomy. Unfortunately, with the insomnia, I had trouble going to sleep at night, so that was when I did a lot of research in an attempt to make myself tired. I had connected with a few friends from high school who worked in radiology as nurses, so I consulted with them on my case and what to do. I sent them all my scans, which were about twenty-five at the time. I had them review all of them. They suggested I come in to let the head radiologist at the hospital where they worked look at them with me there so I could find out firsthand what was truly going on.

During that visit, I was told I had enlarged ovarian veins, which were causing me to have a condition called pelvic congestive syndrome. This condition can cause some of the pain I was experiencing but not all of it. I asked the radiologist, "So what can be done?"

He said, "You would come in for an outpatient procedure wherein we would coil your veins, opening them up where there is so much congestion going on."

I thought, *Great. Another surgical procedure.* It all sounded foreign to me, and I knew I needed a few more opinions. I found a doctor who worked on veins primarily so he could give me a better understanding.

His office got me in fairly quickly. Of course, another appointment meant more time off work and more paperwork. The doctor and his staff were nice to me. They performed a vein ultrasound. He looked at my scans and didn't agree with the initial finding of pelvic congestion syndrome, but the only way to know for sure would be through a venogram. A venogram is an outpatient procedure in which they use an instrument to look around your insides with a tiny camera to see if there are any abnormalities and make sure a patient has what was originally reported.

I wanted to know for sure before committing to that procedure. I made an appointment with another doctor, who happened to be in the same radiology group as the first doctor, and he agreed to meet with me at the hospital where he could pull up my scans and go over his findings with me right then and there. He agreed with the first doctor's assessment that it was pelvic congestion syndrome. He explained a little more in detail about the procedure: they would go in laparoscopically and insert a coil to widen the enlarged ovarian veins. I liked this doctor. He was nice and had a great bedside manner that impressed me.

He assured me that it was a simple procedure, and he believed it would take care of my pain once and for all. I asked him several times about my spine. "So you believe it's not my spine and the hardware but this pelvic congestion syndrome that is giving me problems?"

He replied, "Yes, I am sure one hundred percent."

I was still on the fence about the procedure, but I went ahead and scheduled it for a few weeks out anyway. I thought that by doing so, I had time to get a few more opinions and do more research and could always cancel the procedure. His nurse called the following day to put it on the schedule and get all of my insurance information.

I checked references and reviews, and all of that checked out fine. I went back to see him two weeks before the procedure just to make sure he was positive I had the condition he thought I did. He still felt sure that my veins were congested and that coiling them would help my pain.

April 2016 arrived. My spine-revision surgery was still scheduled, but I thought if I could get pain relief from the vein issue, then I could re- schedule the spine surgery if need be or possibly cancel it altogether. I thought it was important that I know for sure before I went in for a surgical procedure that I might not need. This radiologist also felt it was not my spine at all; he believed the pain was coming from the veins.

Surgery day arrived. I arrived at the hospital at six o'clock in the morning. I was one of the first ones there, so I should have been the first one called back. I got prepped for the procedure right away. I waited for an hour, and nothing happened. I waited for another hour— nothing. After waiting for three hours, I finally asked the nurse, "What in the world is going on? I have been waiting forever!"

She told me it shouldn't be that much longer; the surgeon was running behind. My immediate thought was *How can he be running behind? I was the first one here. Even if he is running behind, three hours?*

I finally got called back. Once I made it to the operating room, I noticed there were at least ten other doctors in the room. All were standing around steadily talking. The attending nurse said to me, "Do you hear them? They are talking about you. That's your case they are talking about." Why I did not get up and walk out I will never understand, but I didn't. I stayed there.

Finally, the doctor came over to me and said, "Mrs. Thomas, you see all these doctors in here? They are so perplexed by your case that they are all waiting to see how your case turns out. You don't have pelvic congestion syndrome like I thought. You have May-Thurners syndrome." He went on to explain that with that condition, pelvic veins were compressed, causing pain and a blockage. Pelvic congestion syndrome demonstrated enlarged pelvic veins, which caused increased pelvic pain. After the explanation, he said, "So since there appears to be a blockage, I am going to put in a stent. This should take care of your pain."

After the stent was in place, I was still pretty out of it. My husband took me home. I had the weekend to recover. By Monday, I was back at work and doubled over in pain. During my lunch hour that day, I drove myself to the hospital to find out why I was in so much pain. The doctor who had done the procedure wasn't there, but another doctor was.

He examined me and said, "Well, you don't appear to have any blood clots, so I will have your doctor call you tomorrow."

Still in pain, I went back to work. The doctor called the next day and wanted to do a venogram. He wanted to be the one to do it. My head was telling me to ask for another doctor, but I didn't. I just said, "Whatever."

I went back to the hospital a few days later for the scheduled venogram. This time, my dad went with me. The doctor came back after it was over and said, "You don't appear to have anything going on that is vein-related, so I think it might be your spine after all."

I said, "But you assured me it was vein-related, and you were adamant it wasn't my spine. Now you're telling me it is?" He went on to say a few more things, but by then, I was just done and over it.

I felt he was in way over his head and didn't have a clue what was really going on with me. Of course, I was devastated that after two more procedures, I was no further along and certainly not pain free. It was becoming a vicious cycle: just when I thought I had found a doctor who could give me a proper diagnosis, I found myself in more pain than before and had no idea why.

A few days passed, and I got an unexpected phone call. I was at work, and I got a call from the doctor's office saying that I was no longer under the previous doctor's care. I was now under the care of another doctor, and I needed to be at the hospital the following Wednesday for another procedure. Apparently, the new doctor felt the stent wasn't long enough and needed to be extended. I didn't know what to think or believe at that point. I just knew I was in pain and was willing to do anything to be out of it. That included going for another procedure. After all, I was just following the doctors' instructions and trusting that they knew what they were doing.

Wednesday finally came. I got up early and went to the hospital for the procedure, praying all the way there that this would be it.

The doctor was nice and had a good bedside manner, as the previous doctor had had, but this doctor was a

51

little different because he not only had come highly recommended, but also supposedly had performed many procedures dealing with veins and conditions that affected the veins, such as mine.

After the procedure was over, the doctor told me he had gone in and basically extended the stent in the left iliac vein, making a larger pathway for blood flow. Unfortunately, the doctor had to rush off to another case, so he was not able to come see me after recovery.

At one point, I heard my sweet dad, who'd come with me since my husband had a work obligation that he could not miss, so my dad accompanied me to the procedure, he told one of the nurses, "I would give anything to get her out of pain."

Once I recovered from the procedure and was discharged, I went home. I took off work the next day in case I needed longer to recover. I had brief moments when the pain lessened, but it never seemed to go away altogether. By that weekend, the pain was back as it had been before the procedures. This time, I didn't go to the hospital or call the doctor's office. I thought I would give it more time and wait until I had my postoperative appointment. One thing I found strange was that before the appointment, I received a card in the mail reminding me of a follow-up appointment with the doctor who'd removed himself from my health case.

Obviously, I disregarded the appointment card since he was no longer part of my case. I did, however, go to the follow-up appointment with the doctor who'd extended the stent. He wanted to know if my pain was any better. I knew I had to be honest with him, so I said, "No, not really. The pain came right back. Maybe not as severe, but it came back." I asked him why the other doctor had left my case without warning or just cause, but he couldn't answer me. He did advise me to give it more time.

I also asked why I hadn't been stented properly the first time. I was thinking, *Dude, it's been a month. I should be way better by now, and I am not. If anything, I'm worse.*

He couldn't answer any of the tough questions I had. That silence, though, told a great deal. I left thinking, *I know exactly why he couldn't answer me. Doctors take up for each other, and they knew it might be a lawsuit waiting to happen.* I left there in a somber mood, knowing the stent of the iliac vein had not worked, but at least I still had the spine surgery scheduled. There was still hope.

By that time, I was still a month and a half away from the spine-revision surgery. I was still having hot flashes, insomnia, and weight gain from the hysterectomy. I was desperate to at least get rid of one ailment or discomfort. I had someone tell me about another gynecologist in the Memphis area. She was supposedly the hormone guru.

I went to see her, and we discussed my spine, leg, and pelvic pain. She thought the pain definitely was coming from my spine. We talked about how my hormones were all over the place with the symptoms and side effects of the hysterectomy, so she immediately put me on hormone shots. She was fully aware I was having a spine surgery in a month, but she didn't seem concerned. I got the first round of shots a month before spine surgery. She explained that I would come just once a month. I saw a difference immediately. The hot flashes were gone.

I thought if nothing else, at least I had a break from the hot flashes. It was now June and time for surgery preop testing. I went for an x-ray, and I saw all the radiologists gather around, so I knew something was up; I just didn't know what. I went straight to my spine surgeon's office. I'll never forget his words. He told me, "Your rods are broken."

I was in complete shock. *How did this happen? How can titanium rods break?* I started reliving moments in my head, wondering, *Was it this or that?* At that moment, I felt a small sense of relief. I finally had a pain source. After an entire year of pain, tears, and frustration, I finally had it, or did I?

My entire drive home, I thought, *This is unbelievable. Broken rods? Broken? Wow!* My next thought was *Hurry up, surgery date, so I can get this fixed.* I just wanted out of pain.

July 2016 finally arrived. The day had come. It was time for my second spine surgery. My cousins came from Arkansas to be with my mom and dad on the day of the surgery. I am not sure if I ever told them this, but their being there meant so much to me, and I know it did to my parents as well. It would take about eight hours to get all the rods out and replaced. That surgery day felt much different from the day of the first surgery. I remember being wheeled into the operating room. I didn't remember that from the first surgery because the anesthesia they give you gives you amnesia. Due to the type of anesthesia, you don't remember much; however, I do remember being wheeled in and hearing music playing, and I had warm blankets on, as it was freezing in there. I said a quick prayer: *God, please let this surgery work. Please let this take care of my pain. If this is not your will, please call me home.* I didn't think I could handle much more pain. After that silent prayer, that was all she wrote. I was out, and it was up to God now.

Many hours later, I was back in my hospital room, and I was in some pain. Spine surgery is no joke. I was hooked up to a morphine pump. I remember my mom, dad, and husband coming in and kissing me on the forehead, and my mom said, "Nikki, Mom's here." I was out again off and on.

As the days moved forward through recovery, I faced pain and more pain. After every single surgery, I got sick from the anesthesia and the meds they gave me. Spine surgery and throwing up do not mix well. When you have spine surgery, the last thing you want to do is vomit. Needless to say, I didn't want to eat anything at all. At one point on day two, the guy from PT showed up.

I was more or less in a quiet state of mind. I didn't want to eat or sit up, and I definitely did not want to walk. All I could do was lie there looking straight ahead. This concerned many at the time. It was almost as if the room were spinning, and I was just sitting there watching it happen.

After the third and fourth days of recovery, I was able to get up and move about a little more. Somehow, I knew inside I was struggling with pain and sadness. I knew the work that lay before me. I knew that in just a few short days, it would be time to leave the hospital, and the real work would begin. That scared me to death.

Time progressed to what I knew would be my last day. I was not ready to leave the hospital. I knew something was off, but I couldn't put my finger on it.

My doctor insisted I was ready. He said, "Nikki, you've done this before. You can do this." For whatever reason, he did not want me to stay an extra day, even though I begged.

I thought, *You have to do what the doctors say. You have to trust they know what is best.* I was about to come home for what I knew would be a long recovery. I was nervous about going home because anything could happen, but ultimately, my fear was *What if this pain comes back? It has before, so what would stop it now?* I just had to trust the process and have hope and faith that all would be alright.

I came home on a Friday and slept most of the weekend. My husband recalled that on Sunday I slept a lot and didn't eat much of anything. Little did I know when I went to bed on Sunday night that I would wake up and see my life take a turn for the worse. I didn't know, but there was one person who did: God knew what I was about to face. He knew what I was facing, and I was in for the fight of my life.

I fell asleep watching a movie.

CHAPTER 5

Code Blue

It was so late that I fell asleep in a big chair in our hearth room, where the television is. When I awoke the next morning, my mother was walking in the door as I was waking up. She was going to get her nails done, and the salon wasn't open yet. She said, "God just led me here to check on you." As I was coming to and starting to move around, I looked down at the most horrible sight: my right leg was as big as a house. It was completely swollen from my femur all the way down to my right foot. My mother, being a retired nurse, immediately looked at it when I said, "Mama, I think my leg is swollen."

She felt my leg, and it was hot to the touch. She said, "Oh my God, you have a blood clot. We have to get you to the hospital."

I told her to call my doctors and ask them what to do. She then called my dad to come pick us up. Our babysitter helped my mom get me dressed as quickly as she could, as I couldn't walk due to the swollen leg. My dad showed up, and he and my mom helped me get in the car, and off to hospital we went. When we arrived, my parents knew I couldn't walk, so they pulled up front to the emergency room door and got a wheelchair. After I was wheeled inside, they took me right back to a room and started hooking me up to every machine known to man. Everything was happening so fast I could hardly keep up.

After a few hours had passed, they took me back for an ultrasound, and the nurse who performed the imaging had a look on her face. I looked up at her with tears in my eyes and said, "Look, I know you aren't supposed to tell me what you just saw, but please tell me. Please don't make me wait on the doctor."

She looked at me and said, "Mrs. Thomas, I am so sorry to tell you this. You have a blood clot the entire length of your right leg and blood clots in each lung."

The world stopped. *What? How can this be? Just a few hours ago, I only had one, and now I have three blood clots total?* My leg hurt badly. I was rolled back to my hospital room.

My husband arrived, and I could see the scared look on his face. To know my husband is to love him. He is a giant teddy bear who makes people laugh. He's hardly ever serious, but this time, he was. Nurses were coming left and right. My vital signs were being checked. This doctor and that doctor, the head pharmacist, and numerous other people were coming to see me. By then, word had circulated that I had been admitted to the hospital with blood clots, and I was placed in the intensive care unit. We all knew what ICU meant: it was serious. Right after I was put in the ICU, I got a nurse named Robert. He was from Africa. He was caring and attentive to me.

I was monitored regularly. Keep in mind that I was only two weeks postop at that point. I was still having pain from my incision, and now this. I didn't understand. It all felt like a whirlwind.

While I was in the ICU, my parents came to see me, and as I remember, two of my children; Owen and Anna-Reeese came to see me as well. I could hardly speak. I knew that no matter what, I had to be strong and not shed one tear in front of them. I could see in their little eyes how scared they were. They had to see their mommy hooked up to all kinds of machines, with tubes going everywhere. I knew they didn't understand what was happening. That moment truly broke my heart knowing my children were seeing me like that. I couldn't even assure them that mommy would be alright because truthfully, no one really knew for sure that I would be.

After a week in the ICU, I was moved to a regular room of the hospital. I was put on blood-clot medicine and sent on my way. My leg was still swollen as big as a house.

There were no scans done to make sure the blood clots had dissolved. I was put on blood thinner and sent on my way. The attending physician at the hospital told me to follow up with my doctor. The following week, I went to see my primary care doctor. I could barely walk and barely breathe. I was using a walker, dragging my right leg behind. I was a nervous wreck, wondering who I would see. I felt humiliated to be using a walker.

My doctor looked at me and pointedly said, "I don't like the way your leg looks or the way it feels. It appears to be very tight." I eagerly waited, wondering what he would say next. He said, "I am making you an appointment with a vascular surgeon."

I became worried, nervous, and anxious. I thought, *A vascular surgeon? Oh my goodness. What if he says this leg has to come off? God only lets special people handle that, and I am not that strong! What is he going to say? Why won't the swelling go down?* I did not leave there with an easy feeling at all. The appointment wore me out physically, as I had to drag my leg all over the place, and it wore me out mentally with the less-than-stellar news I received.

It was finally time for the appointment with the vascular surgeon. I just wanted it to be over with. I just wanted to get on with what he had to say and move on from that nightmare. I got called back, and they put me in a hospital gown to do a vascular ultrasound. I had gotten pretty good at reading nurses and their reactions by then. Once the nurse did the scan, I knew it was bad based on her reaction. She said, "Let me go get the doctor, and he will explain the results to you."

The doctor came in a few minutes later and said, "You still have some blood clots. Multiple ones. I am readmitting you to the hospital immediately. You are going to have to have a surgical procedure called a thrombectomy to remove the blood clots."

He made it sound as if it would be a walk in the park. Little did I know then that it certainly would not be a walk in the park. My dad drove me straight to the hospital. We had to stop on the way to buy me a phone charger because the hospitalization was so unexpected that I didn't have anything with me. I called my mom and husband on the way to let them know we were headed to the hospital. My husband packed me a quick bag with essentials I would need. It was supposed to be an overnight stay, but it ended up being a little more than anticipated.

It was a rough night in the hospital. The surgical procedure wouldn't be performed until the next day. Nurses came to check on me seemingly every ten minutes, checking my blood pressure, oxygen, temperature, and blood work. They kept drawing blood every hour on the hour. I eventually found out that they keep drawing your blood until they get a normal reading. I wasn't getting any rest whatsoever due to all the traffic in and out of my hospital room. There was one particular nurse I unloaded on. I basically told her that I did not want her in my room for the rest of the night. Minutes later, I felt horrible, so right after she left, I explained what I had been through and apologized for my behavior. She was nice about it.

The night seemed to drag on forever, and I did not know what the next day would bring. My parents arrived first thing in the morning. Hour after hour passed. I kept asking when it would be time for my surgery. I always heard, "It shouldn't be long, Mrs. Thomas."

Finally, I was wheeled into the operating room. Thank

goodness for hot blankets because it was cold in there. The nurses began prepping me for surgery. I knew one of the nurses, and it gave me great comfort that she would be in my surgery. At least I had an advocate for me to make sure everything went as planned.

I had to be rolled over on my stomach because, as it was explained to me, they would be extracting the blood clots from my calf. Keep in mind that I was only about five weeks postop at that point. One thing you don't want to do right after spine surgery is lie on your stomach, due to the enormous amount of pressure it puts on your lower spine. They started pumping Dilaudid into my IV. Then I could feel the puncture of the instrument into my leg. It hurt. Oh my God, it hurt! It was a sting and pain like no other.

After a couple hours, the surgical procedure was over. I immediately felt sick to my stomach. I told the nurse. She explained that the nausea would ease up. It never did. It only got worse. I knew I was in for a long night, though I had no clue how bad it was really going to get.

I was getting sicker and more nauseated by the minute. They tried bringing me a bag. I told the nurse, "You can keep this tiny bag. Bring me a tub!" I told my husband absolutely no visitors, per my request, and I even asked my parents to leave. God love my parents, but I knew it was going to get rough. When you are that nauseated and sick, you don't want anyone around to see it. You sure don't want anyone asking you questions or touching you.

I felt bad about asking my own parents to leave, but

when you're that sick, you do what you have to do. The nausea was really setting in. The nurse got mad at me, but I knew I needed to vomit. I proceeded to try to get myself to throw up. If I could just release it, I knew I would feel much better. Once I started throwing up, I couldn't get it to stop. I threw up for eight hours. I vomited so violently that I pulled out my IV, and as I was on a blood thinner, blood was everywhere. It looked like a murder scene in my hospital room. It was very hard for my husband to watch me go through that.

I eventually stopped long enough for my husband to leave and go home for a bit to check on the kids. During the time my husband was gone, I assured him I would be fine, but I wasn't. I just knew he needed a break from the hospital, and I wasn't about to keep him there. For crying out loud, I was in a hospital, so I was in capable hands—until the unimaginable happened. My oxygen started dropping, I was weak, and my chest pain was unreal. It felt as if someone with a butcher knife were stabbing me over and over in my chest. I started vomiting a little more. I truly felt it was the end of my days. I thought, *This is it. This is how I'm going out.*

A few nurses came running in and started yelling, "Code blue! Code blue! I need help in room 719!" I was scared out of my mind. I didn't know what was happening. I just knew that I felt helpless, and the world was spinning out of control around me. The medical team was able to get my blood pressure and oxygen back that night, but I'll never get that vision out of my head—not ever!

Several hours later, my husband came back, and the

head attending nurse filled him in. Even though the worst was over, the thought that it might happen again was scary. Now that I was restless and lethargic, the nurses were giving me anything and everything just so I could get still enough to get some rest.

To say that was a rough patch is an understatement. By then, the pain had come back with a vengeance. I had pelvic pain on both sides, leg pain on both sides, and pain in my spine. It was rough and the worst pain ever!

The doctor who had done the thrombectomy surgery came to see me the following day. He felt bad that I was so sick but knew my body had reacted to the anesthesia medicine. The first thing he asked me was "Who did these stents? Who did the hysterectomy?" I told him. He went on to say words that would forever rock my world: "There was no reason whatsoever to have these stent surgeries or the hysterectomy."

I was speechless. I couldn't speak. I couldn't respond. All I could do was look at him in disbelief with tears rolling down my cheeks.

After I got over the initial shock that I'd had some unnecessary surgeries, I asked him, "How? Why?" He guessed that my radiology scans had been misread, and my diagnosis had not warranted any of those surgeries. He went on to say something profound: "I literally just had to undo all of that. It could have very well killed you, and your life will forever be changed."

I asked, "Can the stents come out?"

He shook his head and said, "No, they are yours for

64

life." He explained that removing a stent was too risky. He told me I would more than likely be on blood thinners for the rest of my life. He said, "You will have to watch everything you do from here on out. If you get into a car wreck and hit your head or fall, you could bleed out due to the blood thinners." The doctor told me that he thought I was good, and he was happy to see that the swelling had already gone down immensely. He'd put an IVC filter in my neck to catch any blood clots should I have any more. He explained, "An IVC filter keeps blood clots at bay and keeps them from traveling to your heart." He impressed on me how lucky I was to have survived this. He decided to keep me for a few more days for further observation due to the complications I'd had. The swelling kept going down more and more, and I started to feel a little better.

I started to feel more like myself over the following days, so after a tough touch-and-go week in the hospital, I was finally released. I hadn't had much to eat due to how sick I was, so my husband brought some soup. He thought to himself what I could I eat that would be nourishing and won't make me sick. A little while later,

He introduced me to shrimp bisque from Amerigo's, a nice Italian restaurant in Memphis. It was the best soup I had ever had, and it's a favorite of mine to this day. Once we arrived home, my husband got me settled in my bed, and my children were happy to see me, as I was them.

My sweet mom came over daily to help with laundry, dishes, and the kids, as I was still in a lot of pain and was still resting quite a bit. Many relatives and friends came to visit me, which helped to lift my spirits. One day my mom asked to see my right foot. I didn't think anything of it at the time. The next thing I knew, she called the doctor who'd done the thrombectomy surgery and told him she thought my foot looked blue and swollen, and he wanted to see me immediately.

I was a little taken aback because I felt there was no need to go back to the hospital. We arrived back at St. Francis Hospital, and I got called back to radiology right away, as they were waiting on me. The nurse performed an ultrasound of my leg. Afterward, I sat in the waiting room with my parents. The doctor came out and said, "You have another blood clot. You will have to come in tomorrow for another thrombectomy surgery."

I could feel tears welling up, and my heart started beating fast. Before I knew it, I was hysterically crying and saying, "I can't do this." I was devastated. I knew how sick I'd been and what I'd gone through, and I could not get that vision out of my head and do that again.

The next day, I arrived back at the hospital—a nervous wreck, of course. The doctor came to visit with me beforehand, assuring me that this go-around would be much easier. He had decided to change up some of the meds to keep me from getting sick. He used a different type of anesthesia, and also added some Phenergan for nausea and some Benadryl to relax me. It really helped. I actually drifted off to sleep during the procedure, and I didn't get sick afterwards like before. He was able to extract the blood clot, and this time, since there were no complications, I got to go to outpatient recovery.

They kept me in recovery for quite a long time just to make sure there weren't any complications like before. Before I was released, I was told I needed to come back in a week to make sure there were no more blood clots. Thankfully, the next week came, and I was in the clear. The doctor who'd done both surgeries set up an appointment with a hematologist. I saw a hematologist for a solid year, undergoing a series of tests to make sure there was no clotting disorder. At one point, I had to have a few iron-blood transfusions because a few tests suggested I was losing blood.

They couldn't determine where the loss of blood was coming from, so I had to undergo an upper and lower GI, which meant another day off work and another test to see what the problem was. After a solid year of more tests, scans, medicine, and dead ends, the doctor finally came to the conclusion that I did not have any type of blood clot disorder, and they couldn't determine a clear cause other than the fact that I'd had the hormone shot a month before the second spine surgery and the second hormone shot a week after the spine surgery. After much research, it was clear that hormone shots can cause blood clots. I was told that had I just had the shot or just had the spine surgery, I would have been fine, but the two in combination sent me over the edge.

Now that the blood-clot nightmare was finally over, I was somewhat relieved but, sadly, not out of pain. I was in some severe pain. I thought, *Where do I begin? Where do I go from here?* I went to see the doctor who'd done the blood-clot surgeries and explained that my legs were in horrible pain. He told me, "There is one last option I could do." He wanted to set me up for an intravenous ultrasound, a two-hour procedure in which they would run a doppler down both legs. He said, "There is a condition called venous insufficiency, wherein your blood pools up in a certain area. The only way to detect it is with this type of ultrasound. If the findings are positive, then we can go in, coil a few veins, and reroute your blood flow." What was interesting about me and my pain was that with this condition, the pain usually lessens when you lie down, which releases the pressure. In my case, the pain worsened instead of lessened.

A venous ultrasound was set up. I had to go to another hospital for the procedure. I cried all the way through it. I cried not because it was painful but because I had been on a major roller coaster of emotions for the past five months. I just wanted to know the source of my pain.

CHAPTER 6

Diagnosis and the Downward Spiral

I just wanted a fix. I was willing to do anything to get out of pain and know why I was in pain. The worst thing in the world is to be in horrible pain but not know why. It had started to take over. It consumed my every thought every day. *Why am I in pain? What's causing this, and what can I do to fix it?* I now had a whole new respect for people with chronic illnesses and pain.

I had to wait a week for the results.

It was a week before Thanksgiving, and I was at work late that particular night. I stayed late many nights as I was often pouring myself into work because it was one thing that got my mind off of the extreme pain I was in. Just as I was about to wrap things up for the night, the doctor called. He said, "Mrs. Thomas, we got your test results back, and I am so sorry to tell you this, but your veins are in perfect working order. I know it sounds bad.

We all wanted there to be a different outcome because it would have been an easy fix. It's got to be skeletal. I feel like it's your spine."

My heart dropped. I couldn't believe what I was hearing. It was just another disappointment, another failed attempt to find the pain source. I must have cried uncontrollably for more than an hour. I eventually got myself together enough to gather my things and head home. Once I got home, I got undressed and cried for the rest of the night. The pain I was in was no joke. It was heavy. It was severe, and It was extreme, but the emotional pain of not knowing was far worse.

By the next morning, I had to pick myself up and keep going just as I had always done before. I had been praying the entire time, but I was really praying now. I thought, *If anyone can make this right, God can. God can fix anything. Can't he? He can heal me and will heal me.*

I prayed daily. I prayed nightly. I prayed for something or someone to come along. Ultimately, I prayed for a miracle. This was a grave situation. It got down to brass tacks, and it was time to get serious. I knew I couldn't mess around with any more doctors in my area after being led to so many dead ends. I knew I needed the real deal and needed to get into a research hospital. I knew I had to try to get into Vanderbilt. It was the closest and best research hospital in the Tennessee area, and closest to me. This was going to be no easy task, though.

I thought, *Where do I begin in trying to get in somewhere like that?* It took a few weeks. I had a good friend who lived in Nashville, and he was in the entertainment industry, so he knew a lot of people with a lot of connections. Thankfully, he had just the right connection to get me to the right doctor. I gathered all my records. It took a long time to get them. I knew I needed everything. I needed all records from every doctor and hospital. I needed surgical reports, doctors' notes, and all radiology scans. I finally collected every bit of it. I would take one doctor or hospital at a time and go during my lunch break to collect them. There were so many, this took a couple of months to go around and gather all I needed. I had thousands of pages and a box full of radiology scans—at least thirty to fifty scans and images, including x-rays, CT scans, upper and lower gastrointestinal tract imaging, venous ultrasounds, MRIs, regular ultrasounds, scans of my pelvis, scans of my spine, scans of my legs, scans of my veins, and scans of my abdomen.

I had it all. The collection was massive; it filled a huge paper box. The radiology scans filled a smaller box, but non the less it filled a box. It was also costly. It costed me seventy-five dollars to send to Nashville, Tennessee. I wanted them to get my records as soon as possible, so I even paid extra to overnight them. I got in to see a prominent, well-known physician who was also a neurologist. I knew I needed a neurologist because of the type of pain I had. It was burning, it was heated, and I had constant numbness and tingling. I was desperate to be pain free. They agreed to take a look at my case. I was so relieved. This was Vanderbilt. They were world renowned and had helped many people before. I just knew they could help me too. My appointment was set for the first week of May 2017.

I continued with my daily life with work, taking care of my children to the best of my ability. The pain increased by the minute. It was all I could do to go to work every day in that much pain. It exhausted me. Most nights, I would come home from work and have to go to straight to bed. I would do my best to cook, clean up, and make the kids' lunches when I could, but for the most part, working full-time while in the midst of the pain, all while trying to get to a pain source, meant doing my own research and education as well. I was not only physically exhausted but mentally exhausted as well.

There were days when I could barely lift my head up, and there were days when I pushed through despite the horrible pain. I was now nauseated all day every day. Dr. Gipson, my pain management doctor, was giving me Phenergan for nausea, and I was eating it like candy due to the extreme nausea. When you have that much nausea and pain, all you can do is get into the fetal position and fight through it. Many mornings I woke up with nausea, so there was no getting ready for work when the nausea and pain hit. Luckily when I started this job, I was told I could work whatever hours as long as I made up my time. I can honestly say I did the best I could do. I gave it my all—maybe not every single day, but I gave it my best shot. The days I did have to come in late, I would always stay late or come in on weekends to make up my time.

I didn't think it would ever get here, but the month

of May finally arrived. It was time to go to Vanderbilt. Every time I was let down, I would have a spell of sadness and depression, but I always managed to rise above it. Overall, I was excited that Vanderbilt might be able to help me.

I was there for a couple weeks on and off. They wanted me to have a special test that used a special dye, called a Myelogram. This is a type of radiology scan where they would inject special dye into my spinal canal and see if they saw a pinched nerve, a failing disc, or anything that would be causing my pain. I went on this trip by myself. Everyone I met was wonderful. When I showed up for the test, there was a major hiccup. I revealed that I was on blood thinner, and they had to cancel the test. I said, "What? Cancel the test?" They explained that the blood thinner could make me bleed out internally when injected with a large needle, and it was just too risky. I needed answers, and I needed them right away.

This was horrible. I left in tears, went back to my hotel, and waited for them to call to see what the next step was. I didn't know if I had to wait just a day or two or a week. Several hours later, the nurse finally called. She told me I needed to be off blood thinner for an entire week and come back next week for the Myelogram. This time, it would be done at the hospital instead of a nearby testing facility. Honestly, I was glad. However, that meant more time off work, more waiting, and more time with pain.

I came back the following week. This time, my mother came with me. We came the night before since I had to be at the hospital the following day so early. I had a nervousness that I couldn't explain. I got checked in for the procedure and was wheeled back. They started injecting the dye, and immediately, pain shot down both legs, and there was a pain in my spine like no other. After the procedure was over, the male nurse who wheeled me back was nice to me. I looked at him with tears in my eyes and said, "What if nothing shows? What am I going to do?"

He looked back at me, knelt down with his hand on one of my thighs, and said, "I'll tell you what you're going to do. You keep pushing through. Don't give up, whatever you do. We are good for this area, but we certainly aren't the best in the world. Keep searching. You'll eventually get to a doctor who can help you."

That statement meant so much to me because for the first time, there was no sugarcoating. There was no dismissing of symptoms, just real talk in real time. He was completely honest with me. That was something I hadn't gotten from anyone regarding my health case. At that moment, I knew if I didn't get good results, I was going to have to take my health into my own hands. At the end of the day, you have to take care of yourself, because no one else is going to, so you have to do it for yourself.

I left with my mom, and she wanted to go eat. I wasn't very hungry due to the overwhelming feeling I had.

Everyone knew I was at Vanderbilt for the second time, and it was crucial that I get a pain source. The next day arrived, and it was time for the doctor's appointment to finally find out what was wrong and what could be done to fix it. I had high hopes that this visit would be different from the rest. During this process, I'd been forced to examine this doctor or that doctor and this scan or that scan. Throughout the entire time, I'd been let down by so many doctors promising to stand by my side, and I wouldn't be abandoned until an answer was found.

Every single time, though, that was exactly what happened: doctors promised to get to the bottom of it, and still, every time, I would hear, "Your case is just so complicated, and we just can't figure this out." Every time I heard those words, I was devastated and disheartened. They would send me down a descending path of sadness that this might be my life forever. Although each and every time brought more sadness than the time before, I somehow found the strength to pull myself together, pick my head up, and keep going. A friend's mom told me once that when something didn't work out the way she wanted, she would just yell, "Next!" and keep going forward.

This was Vanderbilt, though. They were world renowned. Surely, they could help me, when they had helped so many others all over the world. However, knowing and thinking that still left an emptiness in me and a feeling of "What if?" The moment right before the doctor came in, I started to cry, and I couldn't make it stop. I was almost hysterical. Somehow, I knew my story wasn't going to end there. I didn't have a good feeling about that day, the test results, or what I would hear. I have always had a sixth sense. I always had the ability to sense when things weren't quite right, and I was usually spot on, no matter the circumstance.

The doctor came in and said, "Well, it's good and bad news. Nothing major showed on the Myelogram test. It's my opinion that you have a condition called Arachnoiditis along with some bulging discs. This is when your nerve roots are bundled together, causing pain. There is no cure. It would be way too risky for you to have another surgery due to all the blood clots you had."

It was abundantly clear at that point that no doctor was going to touch me due to the blood clots. Hearing the words "There is no cure" hit me in the pit of my stomach. It came pretty close to being told, "You are terminal."

Once again, I left in tears. I left in disbelief, with feelings of hopelessness. I returned home, and I was so sad that all I could do was cry. I felt as if God just didn't care. I thought, *The God I knew would not put me through this over and over.* I had lost my health in a split second. Due to this turmoil, I quit praying, reading my Bible, and going to church completely. Shortly after that experience, my husband said, "I think it's time to go see Dr. Lawrence Lenke."

I replied, "Who the heck is Dr. Lenke?"

He said, "He is a spine surgeon in New York City and not just any surgeon. There is a short list of the best spine surgeons in the country, and he's at the top!"

Just hearing those words gave me a small glimmer of hope, but more than that, I realized at that moment that I would have to leave my home state and surrounding state of Tennessee to get the proper medical care I needed. By this time, I was ready to leave. I wanted the best care I could get. I was even willing to leave the country if that's what it took. I just wanted to be pain free and prepared to do whatever it took to get me there.

A few weeks passed, and I knew time was of the essence for me. Even though my husband had a major connection with his job at Medtronic, I knew I had to act quickly. It also became apparent that was why God had led me to my husband. God had known since the moment I was born that I would one day go through this tragedy, and ultimately, my husband would be the one to lead me to the one doctor who could possibly help and heal me.

It was remarkable. I can still remember when my husband got his job with Medtronic. I can remember every project he worked on, every job advancement, and everything in between that had to do with Medtronic. Now I was being led to a doctor who used nothing but Medtronic hardware. It finally made sense. That was why God had led me to my wonderful husband and connected my husband with a great job at Medtronic. It was the biggest aha moment ever! Even though I was in a state of depression over the news about my health, something was about to happen that would completely change everything.

The fact that this doctor was in New York City was no coincidence. I have always had a great love for New York. While in college many years ago, I once met a guy from New York who was passing through Memphis. We became great friends. I visited him a few times, and he taught me everything he knew about the Big Apple, from the subway system to the best eateries, especially Joe's Pizza near Times Square. I also visited New York while in college with one of my classes I took. When I heard this doctor was located in New York and my journey could possibly take me back to a big city that I dearly loved, my immediate thought was *Of course this doctor is in New York! It makes perfect sense.*

A couple days later, I called the office and spoke to the intake nurse. She kept me on the phone for a good hour, doing a patient interview. Once I'd told her everything I had been through, she responded, "Wow, you sure have been through a lot." She told me that the next step was to send her my most recent records, and they would review them and get back to me on whether I was a candidate or not. I gathered everything together and mailed them off. I sent them certified mail to ensure they got them. Then I had to wait to see if they would at least look at my case.

One particular afternoon, I was speaking to someone in my office, and we were discussing their upcoming MRI, when I had a thought: *It's now been a month, and I never heard from New York to see if they got my records.* At that very second, I heard my phone ring, not realizing that the person on the other end would bring me tears of joy. I ran as fast as I could down the hall to get to my phone. When I saw the area code 212, I knew it was New York. This was the call that would change my life. I was out of breath from running, but I answered the phone, and it was the intake nurse who'd done my patient interview just a few months prior. She said, "Mrs. Thomas, we reviewed your records, and I am happy to tell you that you're a candidate for us at The Spine Hospital."

I was trying to keep my cool the best I could. In all reality, though, I wanted to scream and jump for joy. She immediately transferred me to the scheduling coordinator for my first appointment. It was official: I would go in November for my first appointment. It was now July, and I could hardly wait over the next five months.

As the days turned into weeks and then into months, it seemed as though my pain continually got worse. It was all I could do just to make it through the day. There were days when the pain was so bad from the night before that I would have to take pain meds throughout the night just to get some sleep. The pain was real. It would bring you to tears.

Unfortunately, the effects of the medicine were sometimes still in my system the next day, mainly Benadryl because during this time without warning, I would have such intense itching that I would break out into hives. Oftentimes, the hives and itching would come about in the middle of the night, so I would take Benadryl and other meds just so I could drift off to sleep. There were multiple occasions when I drove to work while covering one eye because my vision was blurry. As if that weren't bad enough, I was nauseated beyond belief, and the pain was so severe it felt as though I were being stabbed with a knife. All of that, paired with no sleep from the night before, made for a miserable existence. I knew I had to keep pushing through the pain. At least now I had hope. Real hope from the best doctor! I was headed to New York in a few short months, and I felt this was the miracle I had hoped for, longed for, and prayed for.

If I could only make it to November, all would be alright in the world. I started doing as much research as I could on this New York doctor, and I was confident he would be able to help me. I read article after article and medical journals. I watched interviews and videos about this doctor, his medical team, and the hospital, New York Presbyterian. I thought that talking with someone who'd had the surgery by Dr. Lenke would give me some insight on what to expect. During the upcoming months, I was connected with quite a few hospital personnel from New York. I was told about a hotel in Yonkers where all of his patients stayed. Dr. Lenke had literally thought of everything. The hotel offered a patient rate. My flight, hotel, multiple appointments at this hospital were all booked and I was good to go.

CHAPTER 7

Life Throws a Curveball

I thought I would share a few patient testimonies of people who reached out to me or people I met along my journey. The first one is Anna Kate. Her earliest memories involve some type of ball, whether a basketball, softball, football, or tennis ball. "If it could be thrown and caught, my dad was always in the yard with me, willing to spend hours and hours throwing with me. My parents signed me up for T-ball when I was three years old, and since then, I have been playing softball ever since," she says. Throughout the years, she also played basketball, volleyball, and soccer, but her first love was always softball. She always dreamed of playing at the college level, and her parents knew how much the dream meant to her. When she was seven years old, she started playing travel softball for competitive teams.

"In April 2015," Anna Kate says, "during a routine

physical, I was diagnosed with progressively aggressive Scoliosis. I was past the bracing stage because my thoracic curve was already at fifty-five degrees, and I was told I would have to undergo spinal fusion surgery to correct this condition." All of a sudden, her dreams of playing college softball were uncertain. She and her parents decided she would play some summer ball, but she would have the surgery in July of that year. On July 6, she checked into the hospital for a grueling seven-hour surgery. Her thoracic curve had increased to sixty-three degrees, and she had developed a thirty-degree curve in her cervical region.

As she tells it, "The team of surgeons placed two eleven-inch titanium rods, eighteen screws, and one hook in my spine." She spent the next four days in the hospital in excruciating pain. For the next six months, she was restricted from all physical activities, which was a depressing time for her. "I had never had to sit out and watch my teammates play without me," she says. She finally received her medical release in December.

She was determined to work hard. She notes her postoperative hard work and achievements as follows:

> That year, I was named All District Honorable Mention Shortstop. I kept working hard, and my sophomore year, I was named March Mississippi Player of the Week, Commercial Appeal's Best of the Preps, All District First Team Shortstop, and MVP for my .429 batting average. My

junior year, I was again named All District First Team Shortstop. This got many looks from colleges. I verbally committed to Delta State University in November of 2017, and I just recently signed my national letter of intent to play at Delta State after high school graduation. What was a daunting diagnosis and recovery have definitely pushed me to never give up and always work hard to achieve my dreams and goals.

Not only is she getting the opportunity to play college softball, but she wants to pursue a career as a pediatric nurse or child life specialist. Because of her experiences, she's compelled to give back to children and their families. Over the years, sports have provided her with many opportunities to give back to her community. When she was ten years old, she got her first opportunity to serve. Her travel softball team volunteered at a Field of Dreams game. "It made me realize just how lucky I was to be alive," she says.

Now it was time for me to hurry up and wait. My husband and I discussed the upcoming trip and decided as a family that since it was during Thanksgiving week, I would travel by myself. He would stay home with our children since they would be out of school for the Thanksgiving holiday break. I've always felt that I am independent. This time would be no different. My parents raised me to be a strong and independent woman, so I knew I could handle anything that came my way. After all, it's not like this was my first rodeo in New York. I had been three times prior, so I felt I would be just fine. I'm pretty much a chameleon. I can adapt in any environment and any situation. I'd proven that from the onset of this health crisis that I had found myself in.

Summer ended, and it was the beginning of fall. It was now September. I started looking on social media to see if I could find anyone who'd had a surgery performd by Dr. Lenke. I came across a wonderful person named Kathy. I messaged her right away. She had posted a photo of her after surgery at New York Presbyterian Hospital, so I knew she was legitimate. I wrote to her that I was a new patient of Dr. Lenke, and would be going for my first set of appointments in a few months. She messaged me right back. I was excited to hear back from her. I knew she was someone special.

After a few streams of messages, we exchanged phone numbers. The first time we talked, our conversation lasted for a few hours. She told me she was from New Orleans, Louisiana, and I knew right away that it was a God thing that we had been connected. I told her that one of my best friends was from New Orleans, and I knew the area well. Kathy and I shared our personal health journey's, and what had led us to Dr. Lenke. She made me feel at ease right away. Her health case was a little different from mine, as she had been diagnosed at age eleven during a school screening.

She wore a back brace, just as I did, for three years, but her spine continued to curve to forty degrees, and she opted not to have the surgery at that time. In 2005, she was diagnosed with a brain disorder called Chiari malformation, as well as syringomyelia and another condition Meniere's disease that affected her ears and caused dizziness. Basically, she had a milder form of spina bifida. Her medical issues were a result of the brain disorder. She had to immediately undergo a brain surgery called a brain decompression. It was severe, as the surgery could've caused her to become paralyzed or even caused death. The surgery was a success, as it stopped the condition from progressing further, but her condition could never be cured. She would have to learn to live with the symptoms, which became many.

The disorder controls balance, and she went for a brain MRI. She has to undergo a brain MRI every few years to make sure the syrinx does not enlarge and cause further issues. Even though she was recovering well from the brain disorder, she noticed that her spine curvature was worsening. While she sought many doctors, there weren't any in Louisiana who would take on her case. She was referred to Emory orthopedic group in Atlanta, Georgia. There was a qualified surgeon who was willing to take on her case, so she had her first spinal fusion in 2009. He also removed four ribs that were being compressed due to the severe kyphosis on her left side.

She was only one year postop when she started having issues with her hardware. Due to complications from loose hardware, doctors decided to remove all of her hardware such as rods, screws, and bolts used in spinal fusion surgeries.

After she recovered from the second spinal fusion, her

lumbar spine began to curve below the fusion without explanation. Within a few weeks of being home, she noticed that her spine was curving at a drastic rate. They went back to Emory, and the doctors could not explain what was happening. Her head was leaning drastically, causing multiple problems. Her balance was so off that she had to walk with a cane and use a wheelchair. The pain was worsening, and she became physically limited in what she was able to do.

They went for a consultation in New Orleans, where she was referred to two spine surgeons. One was Dr. Orr in Cincinnati, and the other was Dr. Lenke. She went to see Dr. Orr first, but after that appointment, Dr. Orr suggested that she see Dr. Lenke. Due to her neurological issue, she needed to see the top spine deformity surgeon— Dr. Lenke—and the rest was history. Kathy had surgery performed by Dr. Lenke in October 2015. She had total reconstructive surgery from her upper thoracic region all the way to the sacrum. The surgery was a success! Dr. Lenke gave Kathy her life back, and she's forever grateful for that.

While my condition primarily dealt with my spine but affected other areas and organs, it was clear that our stories were similar in our struggles of multiple surgeries, yet different in terms of the paths we took to recovery. When Kathy told me that Dr. Lenke had saved her life and said how remarkable he was, I knew in my heart that he could do the same for me. Kathy had lived with pain for many years, so I felt she understood what I was going through.

The following month, in October, my family was traveling to New Orleans for my two boys to play in a soccer tournament. Kathy and I set up a time to meet. I was able to meet Kathy and her sweet husband Rich for dinner. It was amazing to meet someone like her. Scoliosis brought us together, and our meeting blossomed into a beautiful friendship. They both assured me that if any doctor would be able to help me, it would be Dr. Lenke. During that dinner, I also was introduced to Manuel for the first time over the phone. They told me that Manuel had been their personal Uber diver during their time in New York. They went on to say how much Manuel had helped them and prayed for them. I got Manuel's contact information that night.

The following week, Manuel and I talked about my condition and all the upcoming travel information. I expressed my concerns about all I had gone through previously—so many doctors, scans, and disappointments. Manuel assured me that this time would be different. He told me how many people he knew personally whom Dr. Lenke had been able to help, so that was comforting to me.

It was finally November and time for me to leave for New York. I felt many emotions, but most of all, I felt excitement. Once I arrived, there was a smell and vibe in the air that I can't explain. There is truly no other place in the world like New York. All my previous memories of the city I dearly loved all came rushing back. I suddenly remembered everything.

I met Manuel face-to-face for the first time. It was

amazing to meet this person I'd had so many conversations with prior to my visit. He put all my luggage in his car, and little did I know he would share his own personal testimony with me, which would teach me and inspire me. My newfound friend Manuel saved my life. He first asked how I was doing and how I was feeling. I expressed to him that I had a fear of the unknown. I was nervous about meeting the great Dr. Lenke and what his findings would be. Ultimately, this was my last effort to get help. I had so much hope that things would turn out the way I had hoped and desired. Manuel went on to tell me his personal journey of faith.

Several years earlier, he'd worked in a bookstore and made some poor choices that led him down a destructive path. He knew that his fate wasn't good and that he could be headed to prison. He asked his attorney at the time to ask the judge if he could have just one day to spend with his daughter. During that time, even though he had been praying that something would turn around, he felt lost and hopeless. He attempted suicide on a few occasions, and every time, something or someone intervened. On the day of his court appearance, a feeling came over him: he knew all would be all right. The judge gave him no jail time and said she would take a chance on him.

Without a doubt, he knew God had spared him a lengthy prison sentence. The experience led him to be an Uber driver and minister to many, telling his testimony. I was in awe of his strength and endurance throughout the hardship he'd faced. He told me, "My dear Nichole,

I am telling you: God is real, and he is going to take care of you. He made a way for all of this to happen, and his timing is perfect. God has allowed this part of your journey to be right here in New York."

CHAPTER 8

Mississippi Takes Manhattan

It was apparent that through my husband and Medtronic, I had been led to Dr. Lenke and connected to Kathy and then to Manuel. My new friend Manuel became much more to me than an Uber driver and a friend. He was the one to give me the spiritual advice that would get me through my health battle.

We finally made it to my hotel in Yonkers. I officially checked into the hotel where I would stay for the week. Right off the bat, I met two hotel employees who made me feel happy that I had made it all the way from Mississippi. They treated me extra special since I was one of Dr. Lenke's patients.

I made it up to my room. I ran to the window before calling my husband and parents to let them know I had arrived. It was already decorated for Christmas. My hotel sat in the middle of an outdoor mall, and it was the most beautiful, magical sight. I was too excited to go to sleep! It was day one in New York. I had to be at the hospital early for a number of radiology scans. You would think I would have been nervous, but I wasn't. I knew I was where I was supposed to be.

I gave my Uber driver the address to the hospital as if I had been there many times before. Once I arrived, I went straight to radiology. It was nothing like I had ever seen.

I first got a full-body x-ray in a machine that looked like something from the movie *Star Trek*. It was a stand-up machine that scanned my full body. I could hear the sound of it going around as it scanned my entire spine. Once it was over, the girl who'd done the x-ray called me over and said, "Mrs. Thomas, come look at this!" Nothing could have prepared me for what I saw: I was crooked like the letter *S*.

I thought, *How could this be? How am I this crooked after two major spine surgeries? More importantly, how was this not caught?* Dumbfounded, I looked at the x-ray technician and said, "Wow, I can't believe this wasn't caught. I have had scan after scan after scan."

The x-ray technician said, "Sometimes patients are scanned above or below a fusion. That's why it's important to scan the full body." She then said, "Mrs. Thomas, you are at the right place. Dr. Lenke is amazing, and he is going to help you."

I then went for an MRI and a few other scans and filled out a lot of paperwork. I could tell the staff had been trained on how to treat their patients. I felt special. They treated me as if I were the only one there.

It took quite a while to complete the radiology part, and I wouldn't actually get to meet Dr. Lenke until the next day. After the radiology scans, I met my friend at a nearby doughnut shop for doughnuts and coffee.

We had met several months prior when he and his wife were passing through Memphis, so naturally, I wanted to see them while I was there. We had a great time visiting. After that, I took the subway for the first time into the city. Riding the subway for the first time made me a little nauseated. I already felt nauseated due to my condition, but riding the subway made the nausea a little worse. It was hot due to all the people, and the constant stopping and the fast pace of the subway system contributed to my queasy stomach. Once I got off, I walked up a flight of stairs that took me right into Times Square in Manhattan. It was all lit up. I was led straight to Joe's Pizza.

There were huge signs, lights, music, and people everywhere. It truly is the city that doesn't sleep. I had some real New York pizza, and then I just walked around and saw the sights until the pain got the best of me, and I made my way back to my hotel.

On day two, it was time for me to finally meet the entire medical team at the Spine Hospital and the great Dr. Lawrence Lenke. Waiting on Dr. Lenke was kind of like waiting on the Wizard of Oz. I had to fill out more paperwork while waiting on Dr. Lenke. I got a first glimpse of him in the hallway, and I silently squealed with joy. There were at least six other doctors, called fellows, with him. They were like understudies for Dr. Lenke.

It was finally time for me to get called back. I met with

the first fellow, and he spent a lot of time with me. He went over all my medical history, including every single surgery, every procedure, every symptom, and every doctor. He then pulled up my scans for Dr. Lenke to look at and go over with the other fellows. Dr. Lenke came in, and he was nice. I felt a great sense of amazement that I had been given the opportunity to have this incredible doctor look at my case. Dr. Lenke is world-renowned and one of the most highly respected spine surgeons in the country. The leading fellow introduced me.

"This is Mrs. Thomas. She's in her forties, and she's from Mississippi. She's had two prior spine fusions and numerous other surgeries and surgical procedures."

Dr. Lenke went over my scans, watched me walk back and forth, and looked at all my incisions. He spoke in his medical jargon to the other fellows. I heard the words *pelvis, shoulder, leg, posterior, screws,* and *bone.* He looked at me and asked, "You had DVTs and PEs?" He was referring to deep vein thrombosis and pulmonary embolisms.

I looked up and said, "Yes, sir."

He said, "How did you survive that?"

I replied, "I don't really know, but I did, and after five blood clots total, the pain all came back with a vengeance. Can you help me?"

He said they would do their best, but it would be difficult, given my physiology with all the blood clots. He then told me it appeared on the scans that part of my bone never had fused and healed, so first, we had to see why the bone was not healing. He wanted to set me up over the next few days for a bone scan. His nurse then came in and explained the next steps. She explained that we had a tentative surgical plan to remove all my hardware such as rods, screws, and bolts typically used in spinal fusion surgeries and replace it with new instrumentation. We couldn't set a date just yet because he wanted to get the bone scan results back, and we would go from there.

I was relieved that we somewhat had a pain source and had a plan. I had a new fear that I had felt many times before: *When will the bone scan be? When I have the bone scan, what if nothing shows? Surely it will. That's the one scan I've never gotten, so surely I didn't come all this way for nothing to show. I must keep the faith.* With all the unknowns, I had no idea at the time how stressful it would be over the next few days, but I had to keep praying. I had to keep the faith. I just knew God had brought me to this devastating condition and health crisis, and he would get me through it. I got my photo with Dr. Lenke, and he complimented me on my sweater, which made me smile. It was the best day of my life.

I knew I was with the right doctor, and one way or another, I would get the help I had desired so many times before. I was at the hospital nearly all day. By the time I left, it was getting dark outside. I took the subway back into the city so I could relax and breathe in some New York City air. Once the subway got to the first stop, a girl stopped me and said she recognized me from the hospital. She'd had the surgery a year prior and was there for her one-year postop checkup. I thought, *I sure* hope *that is me in a year.* She was with her mother, and they, along with many others, told me that Dr. Lenke was the best of the best and would help me.

When I got into the city, I walked to the Macy's on Thirty-Fourth Street. It was an iconic moment, being on the exact street where the movie *Miracle on Thirty-Fourth Street* had been filmed. There was a huge turkey in front of Macy's, as they were getting ready for the televised Macy's Thanksgiving Day Parade. I then heard a familiar sound: cheerleaders with pom-poms. That was a moment I'll never forget. I was in New York City, being seen by the top spine surgeon in the country due to an injury that had happened many years ago when I was a cheerleader. I've always loved the sport and watching the sport.

Once you're a cheerleader, you're always a cheerleader. I stood there watching them rehearse their routine for the parade in a few days. It took me back as I watched the tight motions, dance moves, smiles, and facial expressions. It sure made for a happy ending to a great day in the Big Apple.

The next day, it was cold and rainy, so I just hung out at my hotel, waiting on Dr. Lenke's office to call with a time and day for the bone scan. I was told there might be a few hiccups with getting me in quickly and with insurance approval since it was a holiday. I waited nearly all day and never heard anything, so I called for an Uber to take me back to the hospital. I thought maybe if I went there, I could find out myself. I had learned the hard way that sometimes you have to take matters into your own hands.

I needed the scan done while I was there in New York to keep from missing more work. I went to the hospital and saw the girl who had worked with me the day before with physical therapy. She had on a blue elephant necklace that would ultimately give me some spiritual guidance once I arrived back home. She told me where to buy the necklace in Bryant Park. She even told me, "You need this necklace, as elephants symbolize strength and good luck." I went up to the Spine Hospital's office with her. I explained I was there to see if I could find out if Dr. Lenke had written the order for the bone scan yet and if she knew when and where it would be.

She was able to find out that Dr. Lenke had indeed written the bone scan order. That was great news.

The next day was Thanksgiving Day. It was beautiful and cold in New York. I mustered up enough energy to brave the cold and go to the Macy's Thanksgiving Day Parade. The floats were amazing! I met some nice people along the parade route who were visiting just as I was. There's something about New York that makes me feel at peace. I loved it. It was awesome to be there for the holidays. Everything was lit up and beautiful.

Whenever I started to hurt due to all the walking, I would take breaks at Starbucks so I could charge my phone and recharge myself enough to keep going. I went on my way to wait for the nurse to call with an appointment time. While I was waiting, a good friend called me and wanted to meet up. This was another family I had met while they were traveling through Memphis earlier that summer. They drove from their home a couple hours away and met me at the hospital. I thought they were taking me to go out to eat, but they ended up taking me to their amazing home about an hour away.

They lived around the Long Island, New York, area. They treated me wonderfully. We had dinner and went to the Hamptons, and they showed me around their beautiful home. It was a nice distraction while waiting on the bone scan to be scheduled. I'll never forget my time with that special family. We will stay in touch forever.

Thanksgiving had come and gone, and I went back to the hospital for my last time. They were able to get me in for a bone scan before I flew back home. I had to go to another hospital to have the bone scan completed. I felt it was important that I get the scan done in New York for a couple reasons. I knew Dr. Lenke would get the results right away, and I didn't want to have to come home and take another day off work and risk the bone scan not getting back to him in a timely manner.

I got checked in immediately. I had to drink a solution, and I was told the bone scan would be done in two different parts. The first part took an hour. I went to the hospital cafeteria and had lunch in between. After lunch, I went back for part two of the bone scan. As I lay there perfectly still, many thoughts rushed into my mind. I closed my eyes and began to pray. *Please, Lord, let this bone scan show what it needs to for me to get the answers I need.*

One of my all-time favorite scriptures that I often refer to is "Do not be anxious about anything, but in everything by prayer and supplication with thanksgiving let your requests be known to God" (Philippians 4:6). I kept praying as they scanned each and every bone. I needed answers, and I needed to be out of pain, whatever it took. I was willing to do anything to get relief. I had undergone so many surgeries and surgical procedures that had left me feeling more pain than before. I had started to go down a road that left me thinking, *So much for signing on the dotted line so many times.* Sadly, it was true I'd signed and agreed to all those surgeries and procedures, but I also had trusted those doctors.

It's not that I wanted those surgeries; I just wanted to be pain free. When you are in as much pain as I was in, you will go to great lengths to be free of pain. Before finding Dr. Lenke, I was considering leaving the country if I had to just to get the help I desired.

The bone scan was finally over. It was a long procedure, so I was at the hospital all day long. I had my luggage in hand, and now it was rush hour. I told the Uber driver to drive as fast as he possibly could to get me to the airport. I closed my eyes and held on for dear life. Everything you've always heard about the crazy traffic in New York is true. It's fast paced, whether you are walking, riding a bike, or taking some other form of transportation.

I made it to the airport, got checked in, and walked as fast as I could to make it to my gate. I had a few minutes to spare before I made the flight back home to Memphis and back to life after my whirlwind trip to New York. Even though I was a bit nervous awaiting the bone scan results, I had a sense of joy that I finally had found some answers, found the right doctor, and had the time of my life in New York. I've always joked that I am a city girl trapped in a country girl's body! I have a thick southern accent, so oftentimes, people assume I am country, listen to country music, and own several pairs of cowgirl boots. It's actually the opposite. I am from the South, but I love big cities. I rarely listen to country music, and I don't own any cowgirl boots.

Music had been my saving grace throughout my health crisis. Christian music especially not only became an outlet for me but also was inspiring. I was constantly introduced to up-and-coming Christian artists who became a winding road map of my life. The lyrics, melodies, and overall messages of some of the songs had a profound impact on me and the way I viewed my life and what was happening. Music got me through some difficult times for sure.

There were many times when I lived in my headphones with music blaring to drown out the noise, negativity, and pain that surrounded me. There came a point when the pain consumed my every thought. I had my family and many friends there to support me, and they got me through some difficult times. On the other hand, there were those who made it difficult for me during the most trying season of my life. I was subjected to looks, remarks, and other indescribable treatment that caused me much distress, including from people I once had considered friends. I thought to myself, *Surely these difficult people know what I am going through. Do they really understand?*

After all, I looked normal on the outside, but on

the inside, it was a different picture. That was hard for people to digest. When I told people I had a debilitating condition, they almost always were in shock. You can't see pain. You can't see discomfort, and you can't see the emotional scars that suffering leaves behind. You can try your best to describe your pain to people, but unless they have actually walked in your shoes, they don't understand. They don't get it. It's never been my nature to walk around looking miserable with no makeup and having a "Whoa, poor, pitiful me" attitude.

I thought to myself on multiple occasions, *If I act like nothing is wrong, then maybe nothing will be.* That couldn't have been further from the truth. Pain takes a toll on you and changes you physically, mentally, and spiritually. It changes you as a wife, mother, employee, friend, and person. You can no longer do things that you used to be able to do. When pain gets a grip on you, combined with multiple medications, including narcotics, you find yourself unable to do much of anything but merely exist.

It was now December. I had made a few calls to New York to inquire about the bone scan results. The longer I had to wait, the more I became worried.

I became frantically worried. On December 15, I was expecting the call. I must have checked my phone every fifteen minutes that day. I was going to get something from my car, when I received the call that left me devastated and inconsolable. My phone rang as I was in my car, and it was New York. The nurse told me, "Mrs. Thomas, we got your bone scan results back, and unfortunately, it didn't match with what Dr. Lenke's original findings of the bone healing. He feels that your condition is inoperable at this time."

I asked, "Why the surgical plan?"

She replied, "That was Dr. Lenke's original thought, but he is now opting out and doesn't feel the surgery will be successful."

At that moment, I had an out-of-body experience. I shut down completely, crying uncontrollably and asking, *Why? How? What just happened?* I got off all social media because I knew people were waiting for answers, and I just couldn't go there. I couldn't talk to family or friends. I'd thought I found my miracle, but it had ended in heartbreak. The only emotion I felt was a deep sadness. I had many photos from New York, and I couldn't bear to look at them. I couldn't wear any of my New York clothing. I couldn't even think of the trip I had just taken a month prior, which had been so magical for me.

It was soon the week before Christmas. I cried and cried some more. I didn't know what to pray for or if I should keep going or give up. During that time, I went to a nearby Catholic church. I cried, pleaded, and poured my heart out to Jesus. I was the only one in the church. I cried and prayed, cried and prayed. I specifically prayed, *Lord, please show me the way. I don't know what to do. I am lost and broken. Please come to me in a dream. I don't care how. Send me a sign, and tell me what to do.*

A few days later, the Lord came to me in a dream. I dreamed that my former surgeon and Dr. Lenke had my records in their hands, steadily going over my health case. I suddenly had a vision of a blue ball. I thought, *Blue ball? What is the significance of the blue ball?* It suddenly came to me there had been a purple yoga ball in the office of the therapist who'd worked with me. Then I knew: *The blue is from the blue elephant necklace she had on.* I hadn't even gotten my necklace out of the package and box yet. I put it on and held on to it. Somehow, it brought strength to get me through the upcoming days and weeks.

As I reflect and look back, I honestly don't know how I made it through Christmas that year. I definitely had lost my Christmas joy. I was sad that I felt as if I had explored all my options and seen them shattered. I thought, *Why did God open all these doors only to have them slam shut in my face?* It didn't make sense. I knew I had to make a tough phone call. I had to tell my new friend Manuel what I'd found out. The call went to voice mail. I decided to leave a message. I told Manuel that I wouldn't be coming back to New York in a few months, as I had hoped, as Dr. Lenke had opted out of the surgical plan. Manuel called me right away. He told me that he usually didn't call many that time of the year, since it was so close to the Christmas holiday, but he'd listened to my message, heard my sad tone, and sensed an emergency to reach out to me. I told Manuel what the nurse had told me. I was crying. "Manuel, what am I going to do? I had so much hope, and now I am hopeless. This was my last chance. I truly feel as though it was my last effort to try to get help. Now what?"

Manuel said, "Nichole, you don't know that Dr. Lenke isn't going to help you and do the surgery. It may just not be right now. I promise that as broken as you are feeling right now, God has gone before you and fought these battles."

I said, "I just don't know what to do."

He then said the unimaginable: "Do nothing. Be still, just like the verse 'Be still and know that I am God' (Psalm 46:10) KJV."

That night, I felt hopeless and overcome with grief. I fell to my knees. I had a debilitating condition; was sick with nausea; and had pelvic, leg, and spine pain. I was weak and tired. My body was worn out. I didn't think I could go on. I had been disappointed many times, but this was the ultimate hardship. I thought it was going to do me in. Many doctors had told me no or said there was nothing they could do. My mind was saying, *Why is this happening to me?* I didn't understand all the hardship.

I thought, *Yes, I have made mistakes in my life, but while I am not perfect, this is just not fair. Am I being punished? Why is life this unfair?* Many had told me they would never abandon me, yet that is exactly what they did. I felt like I wanted to die. Life had become so hard. I didn't have a plan. My desires had been shattered, and I couldn't bear it one second longer.

Manuel talked me off a ledge that cold December night. He took a chance and reached out to me. I now knew why I'd been led to Manuel just a month prior. God strategically had placed him in my life when he did because God knew I would need him. I didn't know it, but God knew.

There weren't many people I could think of locally who would have taken the time to call me and talk me through my pain, and he was calling from New York. He was taking time away from his family during the Christmas holiday season to minister to me, talk to me, and listen to me. He was sent by God. There's no other explanation for it. That was his purpose. God had saved him, and now it was time for him to save someone else—me. Every now and then, a person comes along who has no ulterior motive or agenda and asks for nothing in return. This person is a true gift from God.

Manuel saved my life that night. He inspired me. He made me realize, *God's got this*. He gave me the courage to keep fighting and pushing through the pain. He taught me that God already had fought this battle for me. He inspired me to get some answers but, at the same time, be still and wait.

It was soon January 2018, a brand-new year. I had hopes that this New Year would bring me new chances, new hopes, and new dreams. I decided I needed a phone call from Dr. Lenke himself. If nothing else came out of it, I hoped Dr. Lenke at least could answer some questions and possibly give me some guidance on what I should do next.

I received an email back. Dr. Lenke did answer some questions, but there were still some questions he was vague about. He used words such as *unsure* and *unknown*. He did note in the email that he wasn't sure the surgery would be successful due to the fact that I had been put on opioid medication for a few years, and because of that, it sometimes was hard to treat the pain. There was a nice surprise at the bottom of the email: Dr. Lenke said he wanted to see me again. Since I lived out of state, he wanted to set up a phone conference with me as well as my husband. He specifically said he wanted to have a frank conversation about my condition and the risks, benefits, and potential of helping me. I knew there was hope.

I showed the email to my husband, and he said, "Wow, those were some impressive questions you wrote."

I responded, "Well, with each new doctor and each new diagnosis, I learned something new that I didn't know before that had to do with my health case."

Dr. Lenke's nurse called a few days later to set up the conference call. I left work a little early that day so I could be on time for the call. While driving home, I realized we were in the central time zone, so I thought, *Oh my goodness, I hope I don't miss that phone call*, not realizing at the time that they were just an hour ahead. I can laugh about that now, but I was a little nervous and frantic that day.

I brought out the list of questions I had prepared. My husband looked at me and said, "Really? Is that necessary?"

I said, "Yes, I need answers, and one way or another, I'm going to get them."

We had the phone call, and during the call, Dr. Lenke told me he had the scans pulled up, and he reexamined my case. He then asked me what my symptoms were again. I told him pain in both legs and both sides of my pelvis, nausea, and spine pain. He told me my spine was way out of alignment. My pelvis was also tilted forward, and my shoulders were off. The left seemed to be much higher than the right.

During the conversation, he said the most shocking and surprising thing ever: he told me that he thought if he realigned my spinal column, he could help with two of my symptoms. We then talked about all the blood clots. I asked, "Is that the major risk?"

He said, "No, I am perplexed by the leg pain and numbness you have. There does not appear to be any nerve damage. The major risk is that you will go through this, and it just won't help your pain. I do feel like straightening and realigning your spinal column will fix the nausea, and I can minimize that pelvic pain."

I then asked if the blood clots would be an issue. He said, "Actually, no, we will bring you in a few days early, and insert a central line, and we will be proactive and put in an IVC filter at that time to catch any blood clots should there be any." He told me the risk was that I would go through the procedure and it wouldn't help my pain. Then he told me that if my husband and I were in agreement, he would agree to do the surgery.

I knew that was God. Doctors don't reexamine cases ever. He told me he had looked and spent time with some of his colleagues, trying to find the source of the pain in my legs, and he couldn't see anything, but we would go through with the surgery and hope for the best.

He said, "Even though I don't see anything regarding your legs and, as I said, the surgery may not help your leg pain, it may. It could be that your nerves and muscles are working in overdrive to catch up with your tilted pelvis."

I asked him one final question: "Do I or do I not have arachnoiditis, which is what Vanderbilt said I had?"

He said, "One hundred percent, you do not have arachnoiditis, which is a good thing because the prognosis is not good since there's no cure. To have arachnoiditis, you have to have a clumping of the nerve roots, and you do not have that."

I was relieved and happy. Finally, I got an end result with my health case. Not only had Dr. Lenke agreed to take my complicated case, but I didn't have arachnoiditis, as others had thought. That was the best news ever! I knew something was going to happen. I just didn't know what. I never lost hope, and I never lost faith. The ordeal had been testing at times, but I never had expected that turn. Nobody but God turned my situation around. All I really had wanted was for Dr. Lenke to tell me where to go from there, but the call was better than I ever had imagined. Waiting made it all that much sweeter. He had agreed to do the surgery. My dear friend Manuel had been right. All I had to do was be still. He'd told me I didn't know Dr. Lenke wasn't going to be the one to do the surgery. It just might not have been the right time.

God wanted it to be perfect for me and wanted the right people to be available for the surgery that day. Boy, was he right, even though it was such a trying time for me. I still don't understand why I had to go through that time of devastation, and I may never know. The mental anguish was almost worse than the physical. I actually was okay with it, though, because of the way things had turned completely around. I would go through it all over again in a heartbeat to have that outcome. The waiting made it all the sweeter on the other side. I told Dr. Lenke, "I am in my forties, and I just want my life back. I can't do pain management for the rest of my life."

He said, "We are just going to all hope for the best."

I must have said thank you a million times to Dr. Lenke before getting off the phone. Finally, after four years and eight surgeries, this complicated and complex puzzle had finally been solved. I only told my immediate family because I didn't want to get everyone's hopes up only to have them shattered once again.

Thankfully, everything went through according to God's perfect plan. The next day, his nurse called, and we set a date. It was official. I was on the books, and I would be having my final spine surgery performed by the top spine surgeon in the country.

The date for the surgery was originally scheduled for July, and I would go in May for preop. A few weeks later, I got a call saying they wanted to move my surgery up to June 18. I was ecstatic about the date change. My children would be out of school by then, and I would be one step closer to getting on with my life and being pain free. As I learned and have told many people, if you or a close family member has been given a diagnosis, get multiple opinions. Don't take one doctor's word for it. Do your own research and educate yourself. You have to become your own advocate, as I did. You have to take care of yourself because no one else is going to. I kept telling myself, *I won't be broken down to dust. I will make it over this hurdle!*

It was soon April and time for me to go back to New York for my preop appointment. My husband couldn't come until the actual appointment, and I wanted to go a few days earlier to see sights and visit with friends, so I left on Saturday. My flight was a game changer for the total proceeding. I usually fly American Airlines because that's where I had found the best deals, and I like to keep everything the same. In this one instance, though, I decided to go with Delta Airlines. While on the flight, I began conversing with the lady next to me. She was a flower designer and was in Memphis for a flower show.

While I was packing, my sweet daughter and husband encouraged me to remove some items, as my suitcase was heavy. The items I removed included a coat and gloves. I didn't realize it then, but I was going to need that coat and those gloves.

While on my flight, I told the passenger next to me why I was traveling to New York and shared with her my entire journey. She was astounded. Then she told me about her health journey and battle with breast cancer. Toward the end of my flight, she asked what my plans were for the evening. I told her I planned to get settled in my hotel and then maybe try to go into the city. She asked me if I had ever heard of Carole King.

I told her I had heard of her, but didn't know much about her or her music. She then said she would love for me to join her and her husband for dinner. We discussed timing and such and decided that to save time, I would just come with her to her New York City apartment. I thought, *Are you kidding me? A real New York City apartment on Park Avenue! I must be dreaming. Is this even real? It's a good thing I'm fearless and not scared of strangers.*

She showed me around her apartment, and I felt special. Her husband was just as nice as she was.

It was chilly in New York, even though it was April, so she gave me a nice black wrap coat. I was back in my favorite place, and I felt like a million bucks! After I changed and freshened up, they gave me the surprise of a lifetime. After dinner, they surprised me with Broadway tickets to see the Carole King musical *Beautiful.* It was the most amazing show! After the show, we got to meet a few of the actors and actresses from the show. The two main leads of the show, who played Carole King's love interest and Carole King herself, were so nice. One of them was originally from Kissimmee, Florida, which is close to Orlando, so we made the Disney connection right away.

They asked if I would like a photo with them on the stage. It was an incredible moment and one I'll never forget. It was getting late, so we left, and we stopped by an ice cream shop and got a shake with a piece of cake on top. New York started this ice cream trend, and now they are everywhere. It was a lovely evening. My new friend tried to arrange for an Uber or taxi, but we couldn't find one at that late hour, so she offered to drive me to my hotel. I am grateful for such nice people. I eventually made it back to my hotel. She let me keep her coat, as I would need it for the rest of my trip. It's a good thing she did, because I sure needed it! I got checked in and went straight to bed, as it was late. I went to sleep that night with a great big smile on my face. It just goes to show you that it doesn't take much to extend a little kindness toward another. I will forever be grateful to her!

The next day came, and I slept a little later than usual. When I peeked out the window, it looked beautiful outside, so I decided to get dressed and get ready to go into the city. I got an Uber, and it dropped me off at the nearest metro station. It was only a few blocks away, and then the subway took me into the city. I had made contact with my friend I had met previously, and we'd decided to meet at Macy's. It took me quite a while to meet up with her, and I felt bad about that, but it was out of my control. I learned that sometimes the train takes a while to get into the city, making more stops than usual which changes your route completely.

We finally made our way to each other at Macy's. We shopped a bit and walked around the city before she had to head back to Long Island. By the time we went, it was cold and had started to rain. I walked around for a while longer but started to hurt, so I made my way back to the subway station. I got back to my hotel safely and got ready for bed, as tomorrow would be a big day at the hospital, with lots of scans and tests in radiology. The day after that, my husband would come in for the appointment with Dr. Lenke, and then it would be all business with the medical component of the trip.

I started out in radiology the next day, going from scan to scan, including another set of full-body x-rays, regular x-rays, and an MRI. In between each set of imaging, I prayed that everything would go as scheduled without any complications. I kept checking my husband's flight, as he was supposed to meet me at the hospital, but on that particular day, there was a huge storm that caused his flight to be delayed. I had done that part of my medical treatment so often by then that it was second nature. I knew the drill and knew what to do. My radiology appointments all went great. I was worn out from all of that, so I went straight back to my hotel.

By the time I returned, my husband had made it to my hotel. I rested for a bit before changing to have dinner that night. We found a quaint Italian restaurant not far from the hotel, so we chose to have dinner there. The name of the restaurant was Giovanni's Italian Restaurant. It was the most authentic Italian food I've ever had. We had a great dinner. There were some beautiful buildings and churches nearby, so we walked around and saw some of those.

It was soon time for my appointment with the great Dr. Lenke and his team. I was a tiny bit nervous and just wanted everything to run as smoothly as possible. I knew I couldn't take any more bad news.

Once we were back in our room, Dr. Lenke and all of his fellows came in. They went through every scan slowly, carefully, and thoroughly. I had my husband take a few photos of that part, as it was intriguing to me to watch them so intently going through my scans. Some of the fellows had been at my initial appointment in November, while other fellows were new on board. Dr. Lenke described my medical history to all of them. It was always interesting to watch reactions when doctors got to the part about the blood clots. It didn't matter who the doctor was or where I was, the listeners had shocked looks on their faces— looks of amazement that after a total of five blood clots, I was alive and walking around.

I could hear Dr. Lenke naming each tendon, joint, and bone as he went through the imaging. I heard the word *screws*, and I listened a little more closely than before. I then heard the word *loose*. It appeared that my screws were loose! There it was or at least part of the reason for the surgery. He went on to explain the process. The initial surgical plan was in place, with a few changes. They would be going about five levels higher and five levels lower, all the way to my sacrum. He said, "Now, this is going to be a much bigger surgery than what you're used to, but I believe this is it. Once I straighten you back up, it's really going to help you."

There had been a lot of talk over the past year about a neurostimulator, which I was against getting. It was more of a mental thing for me. I knew in my heart of hearts that I could beat this thing. I knew if I got a stimulator, it would be a constant reminder that I'd succumbed to the condition, and I was not willing to do that—not ever. When I brought that up to Dr. Lenke, he said he took them out rather than putting them in, and he felt there would be no need to have that device after this surgery. He said I could revisit that option a few years from now, but he strongly felt, just as I did, that I didn't need that device.

I knew many people who'd chosen to get stimulators, and not only did the stimulators not help their pain, but the leads came loose, and batteries often needed replaced. That wasn't the route I wanted to take. Dr. Lenke and I were on the same page, and I couldn't have been happier about that. He told me he used nothing but Medtronic hardware and felt it was a good, quality state-of-the-art product; he didn't foresee any complications with the new instrumentation he would be using. I asked him about the anesthesia because of how my body reacted to it, and he set up a meeting with the lead anesthesiologist to go over which meds they would be using.

I got my weight, height, and photos done. They had a machine that took 3-D photos of patients. It was unique equipment. It showed everything as far as bones and joints, but on the flip side, it showed weight gain as well. They liked to do that for all patients to show the before and after, with a focus on the spine curvature and then, of course, the spine straightening afterward. When all of that was over, I took photos with Dr. Lenke and his team. All in all, it was a fantastic preop visit, with not one hiccup. Finally, all the stars had aligned.

God was all over my story from the beginning, so I knew he was with me, and when God is with you, everything falls perfectly into place. Preop was a wrap. It was time to fly home to see my children and get back to life with work and school.

Over the next few months, I worked as normal. My pain continued to worsen, but I tried to keep my focus on the straight and narrow. I was grateful for the turn of events, and I wanted to extend kindness and gratefulness to everyone I came in contact with. It has always been my belief, due to my own personal tragedy, that you should be nice to everyone you meet, because others might be fighting a battle you know nothing about.

It was almost June and almost time for my surgery. It was all I could do to make it through the few weeks I had left. I had much to do before leaving for surgery because I knew how long I would be gone to New York. I was also in much pain. I tried stretches, exercises, and multiple other things to alleviate the pain the best I knew how. Finally, it was time for my flight. A friend made me a special T-shirt for my flight that had a spine and the words *Scoliosis Strong*. My suitcase was packed full with leisure clothes to wear after surgery. I had many feelings. The moment I had longed for had finally arrived.

I was up early and ready to go the next day. I had to fly out a few days early, as I had to have the central line and IVC filter put in a few days before the surgery, so that was one less thing I had to do once it was time for the actual surgery. I flew in on Thursday, and once I got there, I found out I had to have someone with me because it was New York state law that you cannot sign yourself out of one hospital to go to another. I had two different procedures scheduled at two different New

York hospitals. It was just the way they did that type of procedure. As the plane was flying, I thought, *Look out, New York. Here I come!* I wasn't scared; I felt free. *I am brave, for the time is now. This is me!*

Once I made it to my hotel, I had to hurry to get ready to meet up with a nursing coordinator to hire someone to be with me for the two procedures the next day. Talk about stressful! I was trying to get there in a taxi in the heart of Manhattan right at rush hour.

I made it. The lady was nice to wait on me in all the craziness. It was going to be an even crazier night! After that transaction was completed, as I remember, it was five o'clock. I went straight to Saks Fifth Avenue to buy a real Louis Vuitton purse. I had saved for that purse, and I wanted the real deal.

I knew exactly which purse I wanted. I then bought an NYC shirt from the Victoria's Secret store right near Times Square. It was shiny, sparkly, and covered in sequins—the perfect New York shirt for me. I made those two transactions and headed to a second showing of *Beautiful,* the Carole King musical. After my first experience with the incredible show, I was notified that I had a backstage pass and would get to meet the entire cast and crew, including Paul Anthony Stewart. I had watched him for many years when he starred as Danny Santos on the soap opera *Guiding Light.* I thought, *Am I blessed or what?* I knew God was rewarding me for my faithfulness.

After the show, I had my purse in hand and multiple photos and autographs. It was a big day and night for me. It was soon ten o'clock, and I had to get back to my hotel. I was starting to hurt, it was late, and I had to be at the first hospital by six o'clock the next morning. I waited patiently for a taxi. They were everywhere, but just because you see an empty taxi in New York doesn't always mean it will stop for you. What happened next saddened me, but it was a part of my journey I couldn't foresee. After waiting on a taxi, I was thrilled when one finally stopped. I set my Saks Fifth Avenue bag down for a minute to get into the taxi.

The driver took off, and I looked down in sheer panic. I started screaming, "Stop the car! I don't have my bag with my twelve-hundred-dollar purse! Oh my goodness!" He took me back to the spot where he'd picked me up, but was that really my spot? Who knew? I was in the middle of Times Square in Manhattan. I knew finding that bag would be like finding a needle in a haystack. I gave up and found another taxi, nauseated and grief-stricken about my expensive bag. My mother messaged me and texted me to make sure I was back in my hotel. I told her I felt sick. She told me I needed to hurry. Little did she know I was sick for a different reason than she thought. The whole ride back to my hotel, I thought *I just can't believe my purse is really gone. All in the blink of an eye.*

I told her what had just occurred. She always puts a positive spin on things. She reminded me that I could get another purse and shirt. At least I hadn't lost my wallet and phone. "Very true, Mother," I said. I knew there was nothing I could do. I needed to make it back to my hotel in one piece to get some rest. I was sad that what had started out as a wonderful evening in New York had ended so horribly, but maybe the people who now had a brand-new Louis Vuitton bag and shiny, sparkly NYC T-shirt really needed those items and knew they would never have been able to get them on their own. What was a girl to do? Go back and buy another after my central line and filter, of course!

I made it. It was time for my IVC filter at hospital number one, New York Presbyterian Hospital Millstein. The lady I had hired to sit with me that day was there on time, and I was ready and waiting for the doctor who would perform the surgery. The procedure brought back some bad memories, including the blood clots that nearly had claimed my life just a few years prior. It also was a distant but vivid reminder of how far I had come.

I got the filter in. I ran a tiny fever afterward, so they had to keep me a little longer for observation. They lowered my fever just enough to release me long enough for procedure number two.

We took an Uber to the hospital where my second surgery would take place. It was time for the central line to be placed near my clavicle bone. It went in just fine. I had one final step to the process: I had to meet with my physical therapist at the hospital for one final evaluation before the surgery. We had developed quite a rapport, as she was the one who'd helped to get me the original bone scan order and who had the fabulous blue elephant necklace. I am grateful to her and for that necklace. After all, it brought me much comfort and peace during a distressing time of my life.

All the procedures, scans, and evaluations had been completed. I was ready for spine surgery on Monday. Now it was time to go get that second Louis Vuitton purse, central line and all. My nurse went with me. We had some great conversation on the way there. I explained to the employees at Saks Fifth Avenue what had happened. They felt bad for me, but they couldn't give me a discount. I understood. What they did for me was even better than a discount: they embossed my initials in the strap of my purse with gold lettering. That was special! They also gave me some perfume for my trouble. I was grateful for their kindness. We were all crying at first, but by the end of the transaction, we were all smiling. Now I was ready. I came, I saw, and I had some fun. It was time to get my mind ready for the big day.

My husband would be arriving on Sunday. He couldn't come early with me due to a soccer tournament. He had come for my preop and would be there for the most important part, the actual surgery. I stayed at the hotel that Saturday and got some much-needed rest after all the activity and excitement of the past two days. I caught up on emails, texts, and phone calls with all the well-wishers. I then went downstairs, got some dinner from the hotel, and visited with some of the hotel staff. I had been back and forth so often that they had all become like family to me.

Sunday came, and I decided to get a blowout done by a good New York salon. It was the best blowout ever! My hair was soft, silky, and fresh for my surgery. I'd been given advice to do that because, due to the nature of the surgery, I wouldn't be able to wash my hair for a few weeks. The incision would be long, and they didn't want me to risk getting it wet.

By that time, my husband had arrived. I was relieved he could be there for my surgery. We went to eat at a nearby restaurant for my last meal.

CHAPTER 9

The Fight of My Life

Monday, June 18, arrived. It was spine surgery day. I had to be at the hospital by five o'clock in the morning. We got up at three thirty. *Man, that's early*, I thought, but I would be under for at least twelve to fifteen long hours, so I knew I would get caught up on my much-needed rest. I had many emotions about how that day would look. How would it feel? I was at peace. God gave me the peace over all understanding. Our fantastic Uber driver got us to the hospital right on time. My husband and I took the obligatory photo in front of the famous Spine Hospital sign. Next, I got checked in and got prepped for surgery. For this surgery, for the first time, I wore a purple hospital gown. Purple made me think of Prince, so surely that was a good sign. I was ready.

It was time for surgery number nine. I had a moment of silence before the great Dr. Lenke came in to see me.

I prayed a simple prayer: *Dear Lord, thy will be done (Matthew 6:10) KJV.* Dr. Lenke came in shortly thereafter. He shook my husband's hand, and they exchanged words about Medtronic. He then came over to me to ask how I was and if I was ready. I said, "Yes, sir!" I couldn't believe the day had finally arrived. This was the day I had prayed for and hoped for. I had wondered about that day many times, and it was there. I thought about the times when I could barely lift my head up and when I was in so much pain that it took my breath away. I thought about all the sleepless nights, the nausea and pain, the days when I could barely walk, the days when I blacked out over and over again, the constant bumps on my skull due to the blackouts, the endless pain meds that made me feel awful for many reasons, and the constant bouts of constipation that made my pelvic pain worse. I recalled the times when I woke up in the middle of the night with night sweats, hot flashes, and burning, numbing, heated pain in my legs. The thing I thought about most was the constant river of tears. Sometimes I cried so much that I cried myself to sleep.

I just wanted relief. I wanted it all to end. I wanted my life back. I kissed my husband goodbye, and they rolled me into the operating room. Before the anesthesiologist gave me meds, I remember asking "there is no music playing?" The anesthesiologist answered "no music in this operating room. It's all serious business for Dr. Lenke." He then injected my IV and that's all I remember.

Many hours later, I woke up in the ICU, and I immediately felt as if I had been burned and beaten alive, as if someone had gotten a hold of me with a blowtorch. I could hardly breathe from the pain. They had pumped so many meds into me that I had a hard time keeping my eyes open. Dr. Lenke and his team came to check on me. He could tell I was struggling. He told me they were going to have to lower the meds some to get me to wake up and be alert.

I thought, *Do what? Lessen the meds? Oh my word. How am I going to make it through with less medication?*

He explained that I had to be awake to be able to do the work. I would have to get up, walk, and do therapy with the physical therapy team and the occupational therapy team. The physical therapy team gets you up and moving, and the occupational therapy team gets you to do skills to help you return to life. Both teams started coming into my room, along with nurses, other doctors, and the pain management team. New York Presbyterian has thought of everything. They have left no stone unturned. They even have a large waiting area for families with big, comfortable chairs; smart TVs; and catered foods, such as sandwich trays and a variety of desserts.

Dr. Lenke showed me my imaging photos of before and after with my new Medtronic hardware and instrumentation. I was still pretty out of it but do remember him showing me the photos. Everyone was hands-on with my care, and they thought it was incredible how much straighter I was. I was in and out of it from there moving forward. As usual, as with every surgery before, I got sick from the anesthesia. Even though they'd changed up some of the meds, there was an element in the medicine that just didn't agree with my system for some reason.

The cycle was basically as follows: pain, vomit, and repeat. They know you are in and out of it that first day, so they don't really bother with a tray of food. That was a good thing because I didn't even want to look at food until day three or four.

As I came to, I felt my legs and arms pretty much right away to make sure I could feel them. That was a huge blessing in itself. That type of surgery is as risky as it gets. It can cause paralysis or sometimes even death, but I knew I was in good, capable hands with Dr. Lenke. I stayed in the ICU for two days. It was pretty much the same as the day before, with pain, nausea, vomiting, and more pain. Thankfully, the nurses assigned to me tried to make me as comfortable as they possibly could. I slept on and off.

At one point, the pain was so severe that I became very lethargic, and I would straighten and tighten my legs. The nurses came running in. They told me they had never seen anything like it, but I couldn't control it. The pain was so severe, and nothing seemed to help. The pain management team were terrific.

The ICU room was a little small, so I was ready for a regular room that felt more spacious. By day three, I got moved to a regular room. Two of my friends came to visit me. I knew they were coming. They had planned a summer trip to New York, and it just so happened to be during my surgery.

I had forgotten my blue elephant necklace, so my good friend Donna went by my house and got it for me.

I was grateful. She put it around my neck, and I haven't taken it off since. It gave me a sense of comfort to have it with me. I was still in a great deal of pain when my friends Donna and Christy came. They got to witness me trying to turn from left to right. I would scream out in pain every time I had to move. There was no way I could lie on my back with the large incision. The pain was just too severe, so I would try to lie on my left side and then alternate to my right.

The entire floor consisted of spine patients, so those nurses were really trained in how to care for each patient. I could hear the lady next to me screaming out in pain as well, so I knew I wasn't the only one. I fought through the pain as much as I could. It was the toughest surgery to date. I didn't like to see the therapists come, because I knew they were going to make me get up, walk, and move around. Dr. Lenke and his team made rounds every day and came to see me. I wanted Dr. Lenke to be proud of me. He had risked so much to take on my case, so I knew I had to make him proud, and I certainly didn't want to be a difficult patient and make him regret taking my case. I was pushing through the pain and following doctor's orders. When it was time to eat every day, I had to get up out of bed, sit in a chair, and eat for twenty minutes.

Those twenty minutes were the longest ever! I was finally starting to get a little of my appetite back, but very little. The pain was still there. I thought, *Will it ever lessen?* It was so severe at times, with back spasms. The back spasms were awful. It felt as if someone were putting a fist into my back and straight through my chest. When back spasms come, all you can do is hold on and try to breathe through it. Therapy continued, and they would get me up and walking as much as they could.

One day my blood pressure and oxygen kept dropping and fluctuating, so they couldn't get me up to walk for fear I might pass out and fall. Due to that complication, they became concerned about my levels, so another team came in from radiology and checked for blood clots. They performed an EKG and a chest x-ray right there in my hospital bed. It seemed as if it took forever, but I am sure it took just a few minutes. I was hurting, and they knew it, so they were doing their best not to cause more pain.

During that time, I got my catheter out, which I was happy about, but the nurse warned me that if I didn't urinate so many liters, then they would have to put it back in. Wouldn't you know that I had to get the catheter back in? Sometimes the medication slows down the urination process, and to wake everything back up, Dr. Lenke ended up writing an order for a medication that would help speed up the process. Since I was eating a few meals by then and still being pumped full of pain meds, I was constipated so badly that they had to come in and give me an enema. I felt bad for the nurses who had to do that. I must have apologized a million times for making them do that. They always told me they were just doing their jobs. I finally got some relief, and that alone made me feel much better.

Day five brought me to Friday. The hospital administrator

brought in a monogrammed tote and a monogrammed robe, both with the words *The Spine Hospital* on them; a basket of snacks and fruit; and a toiletry bag with a toothbrush and some bath products. As many hospital stays as I'd had at various other hospitals, I had never gotten gifts such as those. They told me they really take care of their patients and make their patients the number-one priority. I couldn't agree more! They said I was originally going to be discharged, but due to the complications and my levels fluctuating the way they were, they would keep me over the weekend, and Monday or Tuesday would be my new discharge date.

I finally got well enough to get discharged. I was still moving slowly and still in a great deal of pain, but somehow, I got enough strength to pull it together to be wheeled out of the hospital. I was headed to what would be a very long recovery. I would be in New York for almost a month before returning home. My husband and I stayed at a hotel in Yonkers. My husband got me settled in. I had a hard time in getting comfortable, whether in the bed or on the couch. I was truly blessed to be at such a great hotel because they were checking on me as well and brought me for comfort.

My husband went to a nearby market to get some food and drinks for us to have in the hotel room. I knew I would be in no position to leave the hotel for a while, so having food on hand would be best. I was expected to be in New York for almost a month to recover. Toward the end of the week, my husband flew back home to help take care of our three children. They had been taken care of during that time by my parents, my two sisters, my sister-in-law, and a few family friends. I was a little anxious about being by myself in the weeks to come. However, I felt I would do just fine as long as I took things carefully and slowly. The hospital had also set up nursing care, so a nurse would visit me regularly, as well as a physical therapist.

A few days after my husband left, I woke up and noticed both legs were slightly bigger, but I thought it was no big deal. I was on quite a bit of medication still and had been through so much, so I thought maybe I was not really seeing what I thought. However, by later that same afternoon, both legs were full-blown swollen. I called my nurse in a panic, thinking I might have blood clots, as this look was familiar to me. I hoped and prayed there were no blood clots. Since it was so late in the afternoon, everyone from Dr. Lenke's office had left for the day, so they asked me to go to the emergency room.

I called for an Uber, and we headed straight to the emergency room. They were busy but eventually got me back to be seen. I saw many things in the emergency room. I thought, *Oh my, what characters are here in the New York waiting room.* I finally got called back after waiting on a stretcher for at least four hours. They did an ultrasound and x-ray to scan and check for blood clots. I was steadfast in prayer because I knew what extreme distress I had gone through before, and I couldn't handle that again, especially now that I'd had a major surgery. When the scans were over, per usual, the nurse wouldn't tell me anything. Why is that? I am sure they are instructed to let the doctor deliver a diagnosis, but why? Does it really hurt all that much for the nurses to go ahead and tell you what they saw?

So now I had to wait on the doctor, wondering, *Do I have blood clots or not?* An hour and a half passed. The emergency room doctor finally came in and relayed good news: I didn't have any blood clots. I thought, *Halleluiah! Praise the Lord!* However, he told me I had postoperative swelling. I was instructed to go back to my hotel and elevate both legs as much as I could. So that was what I did. Whew! What a day in the New York emergency room.

My journey certainly had not been an easy one, with lots of meager moments of complications, but it would not bring me down. I had made it through this far, and I wasn't going to give up now. God hadn't brought me that far only to get that far.

When I was just about three weeks postop, I spent July Fourth in New York. It was a neat celebration at my hotel. Since my hotel sat in the middle of an outdoor mall, there were fireworks, and live bands. Despite recovery, incision, and all of that, I went to enjoy a little of the celebration in hopes it would lift my spirits. I flew in my friend Jennifer in to be with me for the last few days. I felt I had healed enough to try to go back home to Mississippi. Dr. Lenke wanted to evaluate me to make sure. Dr. Lenke noticed that my neck was drooping forward. He explained that this happens when your back muscles are weakened; therefore, he wanted me to wear a neck brace for a while to stabilize my neck.

They fit me for my neck brace, checked my incision, and watched me walk back and forth, and I was on my way. I went back to my hotel and began packing for the journey home. I felt so badly that my friend Jennifer had to carry and check all the baggage, but there was no way I could've handled all of that.

When I got home, it looked as though my children had grown a foot! It had been almost a month, and I was finally back home. It was going to be a long recovery, with lots of ups and downs along the way, but I didn't realize that yet.

I spent the next few days resting as much as I could. Now the real hard part was to begin: recovery. I was essentially pain free, except for the horrible incision and surgical pain. I was happy that for the most part, the aches, pains, and discomfort were pretty much gone. The new rods were no joke.

CHAPTER 10

Rods, Screws, and Bolts—Oh My!

As my spine began to fuse, I could feel every inch of the new rods. It soon was postop week five. I was grateful that some of the discomforts were gone. However, one day, I was lying in bed, and out of nowhere, excruciating leg pain hit. I rose up out of bed and started screaming louder and louder in my mind. *Oh no!* I grabbed ahold of both thighs, hoping I wasn't feeling what I was feeling. I was screaming, but no sound would come out. Just like the movies. Nothing but tears came—lots of tears. I immediately reached out to my medical team in New York. The nurse called in a steroid pack, hoping the pain was my nerves coming back to life; she said they might be inflamed.

After a week of the steroid pack, nothing had happened. I'd found no new relief. I didn't want to believe it. I knew it was back. It was really back. This was the worst possible outcome.

The leg pain was back, but at least I didn't feel it as often as before, so I took a little comfort in that. Only, that didn't last. I couldn't help but wonder how long the pain would last and when it would come back in full force with a vengeance. I sat there and cried until I couldn't cry anymore. I prayed as I wept. I had lost hope and wanted to give up. *Why? Why is it back? It was gone for a whole five weeks. Why now?* The nausea and pelvic pain left. Even though I was eternally grateful that those two discomforts were gone from my body, now the leg pain was back. I didn't understand.

Is it too much to ask to be completely pain free? I was saddened by the return of the leg pain. I knew in my heart that the pain would more than likely stay. I thought, *That huge surgery. The recovery. All that hard work. Was it all for nothing? This is horrible. This is the worst possible aftermath.* I stared blankly into space inside my bedroom. *What am I going to do? I can't go through the rest of my life like this. I can't continue to be on pain medication forever. Those pain meds are the devil.* I was devastated.

I faced the harsh reality that I had been on so many meds to help control the pain that include: Percocet, Phenergan, Hydrocodone, Oxycodone, Oxycontin, numerous muscle relaxers, Lyrica, Gabapentin, Lortab, and the most powerful, which also could be the deadliest, Fentanyl. There were many side effects: stomach cramps, constipation, fatigue, sleepless nights, and sleepiness during the day. My life now consisted of pain, tears and sleep. I became so depressed and stricken with grief over that I was bedridden for a good three months.

I hadn't lost my will to live, but I had definitely lost my desire to eat and drink anything. I was losing weight, and I was losing my spark, my vibrant personality, and my urge to do anything I loved. I was headed down a dark hole that I didn't know how I could get out of. I had started to descend to a downward spiral that once again controlled every thought of every single day. It was such a vicious cycle that I had to remind myself to keep breathing. I think at some point in everyone's life, everyone experiences their plane crash. This was mine. Even though Dr. Lenke had never promised to fix the leg pain, I'd been hoping for the best. We all were.

I kept thinking, *I am only five weeks postop. I have to be back to work in five to six weeks from now. How is that even humanly possible? How am I going to go back to work when I am in this much pain? I can't even get out of bed. This is what it means to hit rock bottom.* I prayed harder than I'd ever prayed for anything. *Please, Lord, take this pain away. Please take this sadness away.* My husband tried to make me eat and drink, but I just shook my head no that I didn't want anything. I was in a dark place. I finally would get up enough energy to take a shower, but even that wore me out.

This dark pattern continued until nine weeks postop. I felt as though I were in hiding. I was hiding from the world. It was the perfect storm.

It was time for my nine-week postop appointment

in New York. I was still hurting badly. I thought, *How am I going to get on a flight?* I couldn't even get myself to pack for a week. I needed to do this, though. *I can do this.* I gave myself pep talks. *Keep fighting. Just keep fighting. Head up. Chin up. This is just a bump in the road.*

If I only knew then that it would be a long and tedious bumpy road, and while on that trip, I would learn some information that made me very uncomfortable. News that would cause me to worry while I had to undergo one last surgical procedure. News that would make me worry to the point I was nauseated. Even though I would be told it was nothing to be concerned with, I was smarter than that, and that sixth sense would come into play big time!

I made it to the airport. I wasn't myself, and I knew it. I hadn't even started physical therapy yet because Dr. Lenke thought it was too soon. Hopefully he would give me the all clear for physical therapy. If I only could start physical therapy, then they could fix the pain, I thought. *They will straighten out whatever is going on with this leg pain.*

I made it to New York. It still had the same smell and the same vibe in the air. My favorite thing to do is drop my bags, change, and head into the city—but not that time, not on that trip. I was too weak and feeble. After all, I was only nine weeks postop, which really is nothing when you're talking about spine surgery, especially the kind in which you're cut from right below your shoulder all the way to your sacrum. It was major spine surgery. This time, I dropped my bags and the sweetest hotel manager, Jason, helped me with my bags and brought them to my hotel room. I went straight to bed. I slept for the rest of the day into the night.

The next day, I headed to the hospital for radiology scans. The familiar full-body x-ray had a much different feel by then. I no longer had a fear of the unknown. I knew exactly what had happened. I knew exactly what had taken place just nine weeks before. I handled my radiology scans like a champ but was too worn out to do anything else, so I went back to my hotel and rested for the rest of the day, as I knew tomorrow would be a long day with my nine-week postop follow-up appointment.

The first two days in New York were exhausting. I knew I had to fight through the most important day, which I called Dr. Lenke Day. I made it to the hospital and only waited a little while. One thing I have learned about doctor visits is this: you never know how it's going to play out. It could be an all-day affair, or you could get seen right away. I have learned to be prepared either way with snacks, medicine, my laptop, cell phone and phone charger.

The appointment started with height, wait, and photos. They pulled up my latest scans, and Dr. Lenke would soon come in with all his fellows.

As I waited, I thought, *Just a while ago, I was sitting where others are sitting today. They probably have so much anticipation, so much worry, and a million thoughts. Then, just like that, you're through with such a huge surgery, and you go into recovery. After that, it's all uphill from there, or it should be anyway.*

Dr. Lenke came in and asked how I was. We went over

all of my previous aches, pains, and discomforts. Then we went over my new aches, pains, and discomforts. We talked about what a rough surgery it was. I brought up the dreaded leg pain. He told me he had hoped it wouldn't come back. He agreed to let me begin physical therapy. He wrote the order for me to start physical therapy, and that was all he wanted me to do at that point. He had told the fellows regarding the leg pain that he looked and studied my scans and even consulted with other colleagues, but no one could come up with a pain source.

When I brought up what he thought about my going back to work, he told me he didn't think I was ready, and he wouldn't be releasing me for a while. It worried me because it was another major bump in the road, but I thought, *He knows what is best since this is what he does day after day. He knows this surgery and recovery phase like the back of his hand. They named him the number-one spine surgeon in the country for a reason!* He said his nurse would prepare a letter for me. I had an idea of when he would release me, and that scared me, as it was a good chunk of time longer than I had anticipated.

He went on, saying how good I looked and noting how much taller I was. I had grown a couple inches with that surgery. It's pretty amazing when you think about it. They can straighten your spine so much that it can make you grow! I think he knew I was fighting back tears. When I asked for a photo with him, he said, "You know, I'm gonna have to start charging you for these." Everyone laughed. I think he said that for my benefit. I had never really seen the funny side of Dr. Lenke before. It meant a lot to me.

I went to see some of my nurses I'd had during the surgery and recovery. They were shocked to see me because they were used to seeing me in hospital gowns and not regular comfortable clothes, so they could hardly tell it was me.

It was a humbling experience to be back at the hospital. I received text messages from many people asking how I was doing. I found some of the messages to be very bewildering. Some of my coworkers and friends wondered how the week was going and when I would be returning to work. I didn't have a date yet because I hadn't received the letter Dr. Lenke was preparing for me, but I knew it would be a good bit of time before I could go back. The good news was that I had a little hope now that I hadn't had before. Now I could officially begin physical therapy. I was hopeful that they would be able to get to the bottom of the leg pain and get me strong enough that I could return to work.

As hard as it would be, I was up for the challenge. I thought, *I've come so far. I have beat all the odds. I can do this. I'll start physical therapy, and I'll be even stronger than before, and soon I will be able to return to my husband, my children, my job, and, most importantly, normalcy. I had one thing in mind since this started: I want my life back.* I still had one more health hurdle to jump: I had to have one final surgical procedure to remove my IVC filter. This procedure would be performed by the Columbia Doctors group. Dr. Lenke is a member of Columbia Doctors. They are some of the most skilled, elite doctors in the world. They provide the highest quality to patients all around the world—and I was one of them!

There was a stipulation before I could get the filter removed: I had to go meet with the doctor who would perform the surgery. I thought that was an excellent idea, as I could go over everything with him that Dr. Lenke and I had discussed. I was interested to see if he might have a different opinion about the leg pain.

I had to go to a new facility in a nearby town in New York. When I got there, everyone was nice. They kept making me speak so they could hear my Southern accent. Little did they know that I loved their New York accent as well! I met with the doctor, and I could tell just from my first impression that he really knew his stuff. Columbia Doctors think outside the box, and they are brilliant at what they do. We got the IVC filter procedure scheduled. I was to return the following day.

I felt ill when I got back from that appointment. I had another constipation episode. I was hurting and could barely walk. I had my Uber driver drop me off at a market near my hotel so I could get some medicine. I could barely walk, and those episodes put pressure on my lower spine and made things at least ten times worse than normal. I was able to get some medicine and got back to my hotel.

I was still moving around slowly, so it took me a while to get back to my hotel room. I was thankful to get some relief. I was so worn out from the day's events that I rested for the rest of the day. I had to be at the other facility early the next day, so it was best that I got some rest.

The lady who checked me in was named Stacy. She was nice, and she called to check on me once I made it back to my hotel. She made me feel special by calling me. She felt that everything would be fine. It put me at ease, which I needed. I knew God allowed us to connect that day for a reason. He always knows whom to place in our paths at the exact moments when we need them.

The day of the final surgical procedure arrived. It was a lot to have to go through nine weeks postop, especially when I was put in unnecessary distress prior to the procedure, but each and every doctor, as always, was professional, and on top of it, I knew I had the best care. These doctors were the best of the best in the world. I got prepped for the procedure. I then had to meet with a radiologist, who performed an ultra venous ultrasound. This is a special type of ultrasound where they test your veins primarily. During the ultrasound, I became a little saddened, and the person doing the exam asked if I was okay.

I told her everything I had been through thus far. Her eyes got big, and she just shook her head as if to say, "That's unbelievable!" She looked at me, touched one of my legs, and said, "Mrs. Thomas, I am so very sorry you went through that, and you are still going through such a hard time. This must be very been terrifying for you." I just nodded.

Thankfully, I had no blood clots, so they could proceed with the procedure. There was a minor issue with my paperwork and insurance; however, it got resolved quickly. They put a drape over me, with a tiny breathing space, in order for them to get to the incision site.

I started to hyperventilate a little. I felt hot and broke out into a sweat. I started crying. I had been through so much, and I felt as if the world were closing in on me. I wasn't just going through things physically, but mentally as well. They were able to get me cooled off and calmed down enough to relax for the procedure. However, I was filled with anxiety during the procedure, as I had an idea of what awaited for me once I returned home.

It took more than an hour for the IVC filter to come out. Once it was out, there was a little more blood than usual, so they took a few extra precautions to get it to stop. They took me back to the recovery wing of the facility.

The anesthesia and other meds had really taken effect by then, so they let me rest for four hours. Once I woke up, they brought me some juice and crackers to keep me from becoming ill. When I realized they had kept me for so many hours, I asked them why. They told me they just wanted to keep an extra eye on me and wanted to make sure I was stable. Then they told me something that made me feel special. One of the physician's assistants, Andrew, who took good care of me, said, "Sometimes there comes along a patient who just pulls on your heartstrings, and for us, that patient has been you."

I thought, *What a lovely thing to say!* They made me feel special. They provided such good care that they even called me after I flew back home to check on me. Now, that's what I call exceptional care.

My time in New York for my nine-week postop was filled with ups and downs. It was time to begin physical therapy and start the real work of healing. I started physical therapy with a group of local physical therapists. We started with swimming. I never will forget my first time in the pool. We used the swimming pool at the local athletic club. I ended up joining DeSoto Athletic Club so I could use the pool and other machines as time moved on during my recovery. As it turned out, joining that gym was one of the best things I could ever do. It really gave me an outlet and helped me to get my health in order. Each new passing day, I went a little farther than the day before. I would add on new exercises. Every other day or so, I would bring up the fact that my legs still hurt with burning, numbing, heated and tingling pain. The main physical therapist told me that she felt it was in my connective tissue. After a few months, I knew a ball between my legs wasn't going to fix connective tissue or was it?

A few weeks passed by, and my recovery took a village, including Dr. Lenke, my medical team, and a new neurologist, who led me to a new physical therapist. I was stuck with about fifty needles, and a nerve conduction study was done. It was normal. Everything else had been removed, and I'd now had spine surgery performed by the top doctor. There was nowhere else for me to go. The pain was getting worse by the minute. Some days it felt worse, and other days it felt the same as it had before surgery. It was suggested that the problem was with fascia, and possibly a diagnosis called inflammation of Fascia. Connective tissue and fascia are the same and it is a clear substance in our bodies, like the clear layer in fried chicken. It was thought and suggested that mine was a real mess that had created a lot of restrictions within my body due to all the trauma and all the surgeries I'd had.

Why didn't anything ever show? More importantly, why was this never suggested before now? Well, fascia doesn't show on any scan. I had so desperately wanted this to be the answer. I had the why. Due to this newfound information and research and education of fascia. I was led to an incredible physical therapist named Susan. I went for a couple treatments with myofascial release. She taught me everything I needed to know about fascia. She became much more to me than a physical therapist; she was also a friend.

CHAPTER 11

The Unthinkable Loss

After a couple treatments, I had some breakthroughs with pain, but unfortunately not enough. There were even days when I didn't need any of the horrible pain medicine or at least not as much. I was never really sold on the idea that the pain was coming from fascia due to the fact that I only had a couple of breakthroughs, but that was it. I eventually learned things that I thought were slowly getting better, but in all actuality, I think I was just having a break in pain for no real specific reason, not because it was healing fascia. I was doing my best, fighting hard to stay afloat and get back to my life as I knew it—until the unthinkable happened.

It was week twelve postop. I knew I would be unable to return to work. I wasn't healing fast enough. I was doing everything in my power to get back to the company that I dearly loved. It was Friday, October 4. It was a day I will never forget. You would think that being cut from shoulder to sacrum and feeling as though you have been beaten alive is the worst thing that can happen. It's not. Losing something you love is.

On that fall day, I suffered a horrible loss: I lost my job over this devastating condition which would not allow me to return in a timely manner. This was something I had no control over. When tragedy strikes, it doesn't discriminate. I fell to my knees. The pain I felt was like none other I had ever felt before. A job I'd dearly loved at a company I'd dearly loved forever was completely gone. The hard work, long hours, and friendships made were gone as well. I must not have ever had my heart broken in high school or college, because I learned for the first time what it felt like to have my heart broken. It wasn't a good place to be. It was earth-shattering. I was broken and hurt. I had no answers but ultimately knew that you didn't fare well among your coworkers when you were especially close with different ones at the top. It just didn't make sense to me. None of it.

The job loss is what hurt the most. I really thought losing my job would be the end of me. I thought there was no way I could survive this. I wept from sunup to sundown. There wasn't a day or a minute when I didn't cry. The job loss sent me into another descending downward spiral I wasn't prepared to go down, nor did I want to. I had to get rid of any remembrance, thought, or reminder. I had many reminders hanging in my closet alone. Those went first. I threw away everything. I soon realized the few friendships I'd made would become merely dust in the wind, a distant memory.

This painful process was surprisingly therapeutic. Even though I had gotten rid of all the reminders, the mental pain was still there. How do you go about healing a broken heart? I was no longer part of a company I once had loved with all my heart, one I had a long history with. I had fought so hard to get out of the bedridden state and back to doing what I loved, but before long, this spiral took me right back to the place I had fought to get out of. I thought and thought. I leaned on those close to me. Still, something was missing. A huge piece of my heart was missing. I truly felt that this loss was going to destroy me. I didn't understand. It just didn't make sense.

I went through every emotion possible. Why? Why was I being punished? Hadn't I been through enough pain and turmoil? I thought, *I'm a good person. I don't deserve this.* The pain I felt in my heart was ten times worse than any physical pain I had endured thus far. I was still in physical pain with my legs and now faced the most severe case of a mental breakdown I ever had gone through. My parents came to my aid during that time. I had no plan; I just knew I wanted to die. I thought, *There has to be more to life than this. There just has to.* At my lowest point ever, my mother said to me, "Nikki, God loves you. He is going to heal you. He cares about you, and he has something better for you."

Then I said words that I never had thought I would utter: "Screw God, Mother!" I just knew he was punishing me.

My mother looked at me, shocked. She said, "Nikki,

listen to what you are saying. He's brought you this far. He's not going to leave you."

I thought, *Whatever, Mom. Whatever. He is just like the many others who have abandoned me throughout this health battle, even though they said they never would.*

They say time heals, but that was not necessarily true in this case. One month passed, and the pain was still just as prevalent as it had been a month before.

I didn't know how I could go on with the many thoughts and memories and the loss of friends I had made along the way. It was all gone. I wanted to end my life, to end the pain, but I just couldn't go through with it. I had lost many people throughout my life to suicide, including a cousin I was extremely close to. All of a sudden, I felt the exact pain he had been feeling when he took his own life many years ago. I could now relate to many people around the globe who had suffered so much that they chose to end their lives.

One particular day, there was a huge dark cloud hanging over me. I just didn't see a way out of it. I was overcome with grief. For crying out loud, I had children to think about. If I were to end my life, my three wonderful children would suffer the most. I knew that.

I am a certified teacher, and I had witnessed the destruction that losing a parent had on children. Their perfect grades and behavior were lost. I knew my children would spend the rest of their childhood and probably their adulthood seeking therapy, and my actions would be the cause. Still, I needed a way out. I thought, *What difference does it make whether I am physically here on*

Earth or not? I am alive but totally dead on the inside. In all actuality, my sweet children had lost their mother when that ordeal began a few years ago. Still, I thought of a way out of my miserable existence. I had something that came to mind that I hadn't thought I would ever do.

I thought of a plan. I thought, *I can't physically end my life, but that doesn't mean I can't hire someone to end it for me.* Although the thought was completely delusional, I wasn't in my right state of mind. The grief overpowered everything. I went to the bank and grabbed a good bit of cash from my medical fund. From my time as a teacher, I knew the bad areas of Memphis. I'd taught students from those areas. I'd visited with the parents from those areas, and I was friends with many police officers who confirmed for me those bad areas of town. I drove into Memphis.

My destination was the poverty-stricken, undesirable part of town. I thought, *I'll hire my own hit man. Is that even humanly possible?* I cried so hard the entire way there that I could hardly see the road. I put on the most depressing music I could find. I had clearly lost it. I had lost much during that tragedy, including my will to live. I had failed my parents, my husband, and my children. I thought back to the numerous people who had once told me how strong I was. I didn't feel strong at that moment. I had lost my health, my job, and the many abilities I once had had. My life was now different. Loss can drive a person to the brink and make her feel as if the walls are closing in. My image was painted on the canvas of despair. I had clearly lost Jesus through this ordeal. I needed a serious intervention.

I finally arrived in the most egregious part of Memphis, Tennessee. I kept driving in circles. It was a whirlwind. There was not one person in sight. Then the long stretch of road stopped winding around. I had been detoured. Somehow, there it was: the serious intervention that stopped my master plan of ending my life. I thought the road map of my life was over, but it was actually beginning. I just didn't realize it. I wouldn't realize it for many weeks to come.

I found a spot to pull over. There was still not a single soul to be seen. I wept for a solid hour. The tears then stopped, and I began talking to God, something I hadn't been able to do for a few months.

I prayed, "God, I know it was you who made me detour and cleared my destructive path. Please hold me tightly. Please lead me and guide me. I'm at a total loss and just don't know what to do. I am the saddest I have ever been. Please send me one glimmer of hope. Just one." I pulled myself together enough to make the long trek back home. I made it home and was mentally exhausted from the tears, the sadness, and the events that had transpired that day.

I went straight to bed. I needed to regroup and would devise a plan of attack the next day. There it was, my answer: *There's a tomorrow. There's always a tomorrow.*

I think when people go through major suffering, as I have, they forget that there's a tomorrow. The next day came. I knew God had saved me that night. The events of the day before would always remain with me—and just with me. I knew if I were to tell people—anyone— they would assume I was insane, and I couldn't bear that thought. All the times I'd told myself, "Now the fight really begins," had been just tiny preparations for that moment in time. *Now the real fight begins. I will make it through this. I am a fighter. I am a warrior. I am standing right in the face fear. Every time I fall down, I get stronger.*

There's a beautiful reminder in every scar on my skin. Seeing those reminders made me feel brave and strong enough to fight the fight. As I looked at the sky, I could hear the thunder roar; I could envision and hear the battle cry. I was not about to give in. I just needed to feel alive so I could fight. After all, it's much harder to fight it than to feel it. I had to let myself heal. I had to become a voice for the millions of others who had struggled with pain and conditions just like mine. God revealed it to me. There was a much greater purpose for my pain. I knew I could take on much more than I ever had dreamed of.

I had to lean in on God and let him mold me into not just my own desires but also the desires he had for me. When you let go of God's hand, even if just for a minute, he never lets go. God was there the whole time. I just had to trust. I just had to keep faith. I couldn't just talk the talk; I had to walk the walk with God. I had to fully trust in him. I said, "God, I sure don't know what you're doing, but I trust you." It's the hardest thing ever to put your trust in him, but after losing everything, that was all I had left. It takes a whole lot of faith, but ultimately, I knew there would be a day when my struggle would end. You are born on purpose. You are a purpose, and there's a purpose for your struggle, a purpose for your pain.

CHAPTER 12

Purpose for Pain

There is a purpose for my pain. I went through all of this to help others. I did all of this for others. If I can help just one person, it will all have been worth it to me, every single bit of it.

There were times when I would revisit the dark places I had been, but Jesus was holding my heart. He was holding my hand, and only he could restore what I'd lost. What was coming would be way better than what I'd lost. It was not over. God was not done with me yet. I knew if I could just hold on to hope, it would come full circle in the end. Slowly, I began to get my spark back. However, I knew I couldn't do it alone. I had to get an outside opinion from someone who knew nothing about me or my situation. I had to get professional help.

I had hit rock bottom, and I thought if anyone could help me through, it would be a counselor. I went through a few, and finally, I found one I made an immediate connection with. She helped me realize much about myself. It was intense. I had lots of therapy sessions—not just physical therapy but now mental therapy too. It took about ten sessions with my new counselor. At one point, she gave me some paper and wanted me to write down everything I was grateful for. I just wasn't there yet. I had much to be grateful for, but the loss, devastation, and struggle overshadowed the good versus evil.

Over time, she was able to give me the tools I needed to get over that hurdle. She helped me find the courage to ask God, "What are you trying to teach me?" There were people I was desperately trying to hold on to who simply weren't meant to be in my life anymore. Holding on was only hurting me further. God had put an end to many friendships and relationships that were toxic. I wanted to keep them and hold on to them forever. I just didn't understand. I thought, *How can all of these people I have been friends with forever leave me in such hard, devastating times?*

I had to remember that not everyone understands my struggle or the grief that comes along with it. She helped me to realize that God was teaching me something important. Not everyone thinks like you or has the same work ethic you do. Point blank, not everyone is like you! Those were powerful words and made a strong impact. It was time for me to accept the abuse and faults of not only others but also myself. It's hard to forgive those who have hurt us, but if God can forgive us, we have to forgive others as well. Going above and beyond doesn't mean people will appreciate you. In the minds of others, we never asked for that.

Most importantly, God taught me not to allow myself to think about the why or the what. Others don't have to understand what I was going through. You show others who you are by your character. By allowing yourself to keep picking your head up, you show others exactly who you are. Not everyone wants to handle stress. Sometimes people will take the cowardly way out in lieu of dealing with another person's stress. Sometimes people and situations are either lessons or blessings. I realized that fear was driven by people. I stood up and said to myself, "I refuse to live in fear for one more day!"

It became apparent to me: *I am unshakable. I am unstoppable. I am fearless.* In that season of struggle and pain, I refused to allow fear to keep me bound. *I will weather this storm for as long as it takes. The fact that I am still here shows that there is a much greater purpose for me.*

I had learned a great deal. Unfortunately, some people in this big world have a purpose of making others miserable. When people have that purpose, it's really no purpose at all. Sometimes what we think is our purpose is not God's purpose for our lives. The Enemy doesn't mess with you if you're strong. The message I received overall was that I was strong, and I was enough.

God had orchestrated every part of my journey. He knew from the moment I was born that I could and would do great things. He knew from the onset, when I was diagnosed at age sixteen with Scoliosis, that would become my platform. It would be my purpose in life. His purpose was not to destroy me on the way but to reach me with some huge life lessons. No one ever said it would be easy. In fact, it's been anything but an easy road. I faced struggles, pain, near-death experiences, multiple losses, and more along the way. I eventually learned that just when I thought my life was over and there was an end in sight, it was really just beginning.

There were two significant moments throughout my journey that helped me get to where I am today. One happened right before my final surgery. Two days before I flew out to New York, I got an important call from Massachusetts. It was the president of the National Scoliosis Foundation. Their board had approved me as an ambassador for the foundation for the state of Mississippi. It's a cause that's always been near and dear to my heart, and I knew it was time to start changing lives and helping others suffering with Scoliosis and other conditions related to the spine. The spine is the driving force of the body. It controls everything. It affects everything, even down to the breaths we take.

The best memory I have from my journey is of a special moment in New York, one I'll always treasure because it was definitely a God-sent story. I met an Uber driver on one of my last stops at my six-month postop visit. I had just gotten off at my last train stop and was waiting on an Uber I had scheduled. As I went outside to meet him, he sped off. I was left there with my hands in the air, wondering what had happened. A gentleman walked around the corner at that moment. He asked if I needed a ride and then asked where I was from.

I told him, "Mississippi. We are really close to Memphis."

He knew the area well. It turned out he used to live there. He asked me what had brought me all the way to New York. I explained that I had come there to have my ninth surgery, my third major spine surgery. He then said, "So if you don't mind me asking, why such a big spine surgery?"

I told him, "When I was a teenager, I fell off a three-man-high pyramid and fractured my spine, and shortly after, I was diagnosed with Scoliosis. It was a pretty serious accident."

He suddenly pulled over and stopped the car. I thought to myself, *Oh my goodness, what is he doing?*

He looked back at me and said, "In 1989?"

I was in shock. I said, "Oh my goodness, how did you possibly know that?" He couldn't have known how old I was.

It turned out he used to be a motor coach driver for cheerleading squads in the Mississippi and Midsouth area. He told me there had been a particular day when he was driving a cheer squad to competition, and they'd talked about my accident. The head cheerleader had said, "Guys, we have got to be more careful; she could have died." He told me, "That was you they were talking about."

I was in the back of the car, crying joyful tears. What an incredible encounter. Only God himself could've orchestrated that meeting. That driver was sent to me by God. I knew it. I had never had an encounter with an angel, but I knew God had sent him to me that night.

I must have smiled and cried for more than an hour. In that moment, I realized nobody but God could have pulled that off. I was destined for great things, and it was only the beginning. It was an incredible trip back to New York.

After I returned home, I began reading *Jesus Calling* and reading the Bible verses attached to each page. Things started happening. God was busy working behind the scenes. He had lined up everything in perfect order, just as it was intended to be from the beginning.

I just had to figure it out for myself. This was it. This was my purpose for my pain. I'd gone from cheerleading and Disney to pain, struggles, surgeries, and downward spirals of depression and from elementary schools to big corporations. For once, I was the student, and Jesus was the teacher. I had to learn that every new beginning has an end. I would choose to see the good in every situation. With each passing moment, time had proven over and over again that it wasn't my friend. God's voice was constantly in my ear. He held me up every time I fell. I would teach others to be strong through my story of triumph over tragedy.

I would inspire others to fight the good fight, even when the fight was not there, just as Jesus had told me to do. He was cheering me on; therefore, I could and would finish strong. I held on to Jesus. I kept the faith. I kept running the race. I persisted. In the end, I saw a total transformation take place in me. God transformed me not from the outside in but from the inside out. He healed me mentally and spiritually, and he would take care of the physical. I had had good days and bad days. I'd faced winning and defeat. I'd learned a great deal through the upheavals. When I was at my end, God was my Savior and sustainer, my healer and my friend.

I wanted to tell my story in hopes of inspiring others. Often, I disliked my body, as I felt it was diseased and filled with pain. I didn't like the way it looked and sure did not like the way it felt. It was disheartening that it took many years to get to part of a diagnosis. Amid the scans, medicines, and doctor's appointments, ultimately, I knew that every single doctor and every single disappointment would ultimately lead me to where I was going. They would lead me to the right doctor. You often hear people say, "It takes a doctor with the right set of eyes," but for me, it was the right set of ears. What a journey this has been. I needed a doctor willing to really listen to every single ache, pain, and discomfort.

I want to inspire others to keep pushing through. You might think there's not a doctor who can help you, but there is. You just have to be willing to jump through a few hoops to find him or her. I saw firsthand when God pointed out to me not only the price he paid but also the price we all pay during the storm. My personal tragedy reminded me often of when Jesus was nailed to the cross. I can imagine the sheer pain he was in as each nail was being driven into each hand on the cross. People ridiculed him, just as many friends left me in my health crisis and time of need. Jesus said, "God has forsaken me," and I felt that way as well.

For the first time, I could really see what Jesus had gone through physically and mentally. If you've never been through it, you can't possibly understand it. People that live with chronic pain, feel like it's not just the pain. It is a complete mental, physical, emotional attack on the human body. Sometimes, it's not understood that God protects us by removing us from the equation. I have learned that we have many seasons of life. Some seasons are good and have to be patient and hold on because help is on the way. Be still and let God do his thing. We have to wait on him to work this out. God is simply not asking us to figure this out on our own, but he's asking us to trust that he already has. He has gone before us to fight every one of these battles. Lastly, It's alright to feel your emotions of sadness, anger, and fear, but you have to keep going and you must not ever give up. Through my experience, God will replace with what you have lost with something much better. Even with all the negative and loss that has occurred all in one season for me such as: loss of health, job, and friends. It wasn't rejection, but simply redirection.

I have grown so much on this spiritual journey, and Jesus has truly transformed me throughout this journey. It didn't matter how far I wandered away; he kept calling my name. God was always with me through the trenches. He kept telling me, "Don't stop believing, and don't you dare give up!" God is so good at writing our very own stories than we could have ever imagined. He wants us to empower others, lead with our hearts, and use our voices with our very own health case and difficult times.

There have been many trials and tribulations along this journey. I have faced agony and defeat, but I've come to realize that every dark cloud has a silver lining. I decided to turn my pain into power and my visions into victories. Through this enormous ride, I can celebrate those small victories all while continuing to fight for my right of a pain free life. Now that I have come out of the storm, I am definitely not the same person that walked in. After all, isn't that what the storm is all about? I am still not sure if I will ever get a proper full diagnosis of the remaining pain and health challenge. I'm not sure that it will eventually lead to the right treatment, but I will keep on searching and fighting until that final round.

Maybe I will get to that rainbow in the end, and maybe I won't, but either way, I know God will take this mess and turn it into a miracle. I know that I am here so I can tell others how I overcame what I went through, and just maybe that will become someone else's key to survival. I was put on this Earth to tell others that they are still good and glorious human beings, even in the midst of their struggle. One day, it just clicks. You will come to realize what is important and what isn't. You will remember how very far you have come, and you'll remember when you thought things were so bad that you would never recover, but you did. That's when you smile because you are truly proud of the person you have fought hard to become. You will remember who you were, before, during and after your difficult time, and the game changed.

In the end, I will come out a fighter. There's no doubt, that I was made to fight, and this struggle of pain will make me stronger, no matter how much it hurts. For once, I want to wake up and feel like I won this battle. The odds are very much still against me to be completely healed, but I do finally have the strength, I can muster up and have enough hope to share, reach and teach with the world. I have been on this amazing journey, that is now part of the past; In despite of the tears, pain, suffering, sorrow, and loss, one thing is for certain: I will live each day as if it could very well be my last.

My parents, my sister and I 1977

My parents Johnny and Sherry Manis

My parents and I at my wedding

My parents, my sisters Jenny and Half sister
Mary Jane and I at my wedding.

Southaven Cheer Memorbilia

Southaven Varsity Cheer 1990

College Cheer Northwest Cheer squad

Arkansas State University dance team

Arkansas State University dance team

Myself with dance/character partner
at Walt Disney World

Myself with Tigger right after my audition
and was officially casted a character at
Walt Disney World in Orlando, Florida.

Family photo of my husband Brandon, myself,
and our children Owen, Ian, and Anna-Reese.

My husband Brandon and myself

My children Owen, Ian, and Anna-Reese

Wedding Day at the Cathedral of the Immaculate Conception Catholic Church Memphis, Tennessee.

Wedding Day at the Cathedral of the Immaculate Conception Catholic Church Memphis, Tennessee.

Myself with my ICU nurse Robert at St. Francis Hospital

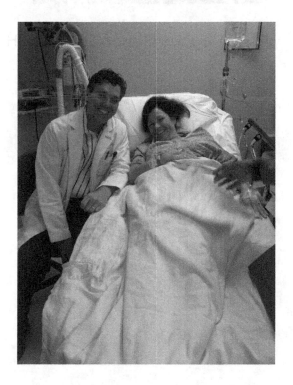

My first spine surgery. Myself with Dr. Linville

Myself with Dr. Stephen Gipson St. Francis Hospital

Myself with my doctors at six weeks post-op in 2013.

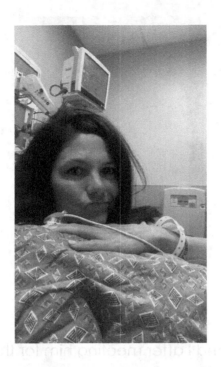

Myself at hospital during a scary time.

Myself at The Spine Hospital for the
first time. November 2017

Dr. Lenke and I after meeting him for the first time after the initial phase of treatment. November 2017

Myself at Macy's on 34th Street.

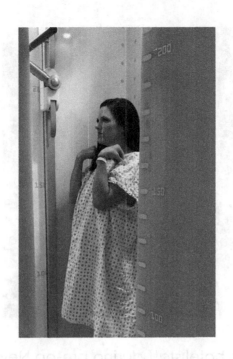

Myself getting a full body x-ray New
York Presbyterian Hospital.

Myself at the Today Show gift shop.
November 2017

Myself with hotel staff during pre-op New York visit.

Myself with Shirley one of the New York Presbyterian
staff members during my pre-op visit

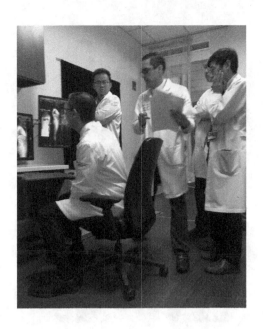

Dr. Lenke and his fellows going over
scans during pre-op visit. April 2018

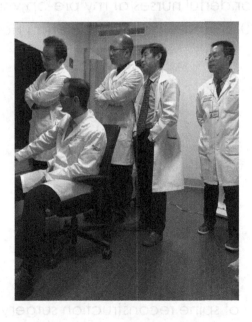

Dr. Lenke and his fellows looking at my scans and
discussing my case during the pre-op visit April 2018

Myself with Dr. Lenke and one of his
wonderful nurses at my pre-op visit.
April 2018 at New York Presbyterian Hospital.

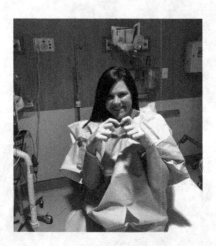

Day of spine reconstruction surgery at
New York Presbyterian Hospital.
June 18, 2018

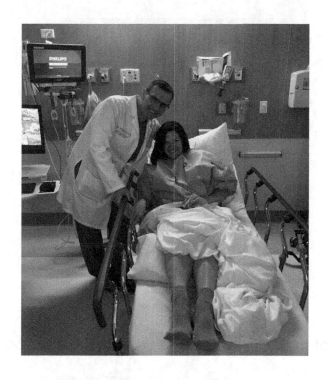

Dr. Lenke and I right before surgery.
June 18, 2018

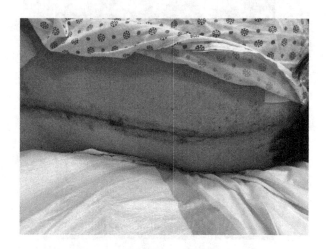

Photo of incision 3 days post-op.
New York Presbyterian Hospital.

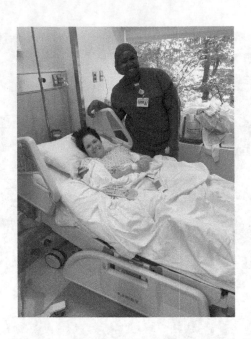

One of my wonderful nurses and I at 4 days post-op.

My husband Brandon and I before
spine surgery. June 18, 2018.

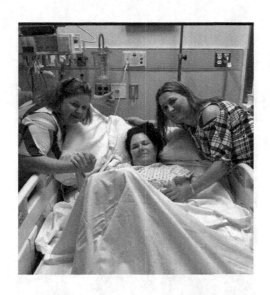

My friends Donna and Christy 2 days
post op. The Spine Hospital

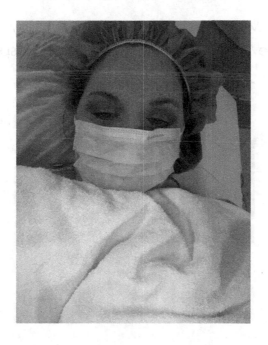

Myself resting after spine surgery.
June 2018 New York Presbyterian Hospital.

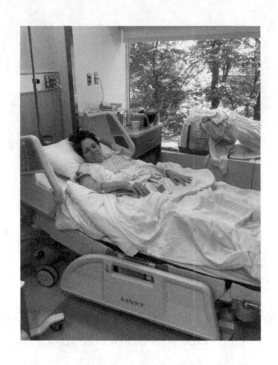

Myself resting after spine surgery.
June 2018 New York Presbyterian Hospital.

Pictures of myself with some of the cast of the
Carole King Musical Beautiful. June 14, 2018

Myself at Rockefeller Center seeing the Christmas tree. 6 months post op visit. December 2018

6 months post- op visit. Myself with the special Uber driver Rich. I call him "The Angel Driver" December 2018

Myself with Dr. Lenke and his dream
team. 6 months post-op.
New York Presbyterian Hospital.

Myself with my friend Annette Brill seeing
them broadway musical Waitress. We
met a few years prior in Memphis.

Dr. Lenke and I at my one-year post op
visit. New York Presbyterian Hospital.
June 2019

Me at the Today Show in
New York City June 17, 2019

Dr. Lenke and I at my one-year post op
visit at The Spine Hospital June 2019

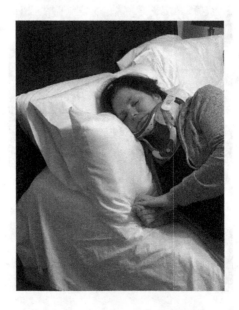

Me during recovery. This was truly the
fight of my life. September-2019

Me during physical therapy having
a Cryotherapy session.

Me doing therapy and training at Desoto Athletic Club.

Myself at my lowest weight ever at 128 pounds. Photo taken after a training session at the Desoto Athletic Club in Southaven, Mississippi.

Left top Myself with The Brill Family
Top Right My friend Christina

Bottom Left :Anna Kate Gregg
Bottom Middle: Myself with spine patient
Kathy Bottom right: Myself with Manuel

My Disney name tag

Myself at Walt Disney World

Columbia Doctors IVC Removall 9
weeks post op (Andrew)

Myself in Manhattan getting MRI at New York
Neurological Institute 6 month post op

Myself with NYPD in Manhattan

Myself on Subway Pre Op Visit-

Myself with Columbia Doctors 3 months post op

Printed in the United States
By Bookmasters